Getting Started with Storm

Jonathan Leibiusky, Gabriel Eisbruch,
and Dario Simonassi

O'REILLY®

Beijing · Cambridge · Farnham · Köln · Sebastopol · Tokyo

Getting Started with Storm

by Jonathan Leibiusky, Gabriel Eisbruch, and Dario Simonassi

Published by O'Reilly Media, Inc., 1005 Gravenstein Highway North, Sebastopol, CA 95472.

O'Reilly books may be purchased for educational, business, or sales promotional use. Online editions are also available for most titles (*http://my.safaribooksonline.com*). For more information, contact our corporate/institutional sales department: 800-998-9938 or *corporate@oreilly.com*.

Editors: Mike Loukides and Shawn Wallace	**Cover Designer:** Karen Montgomery
Production Editor: Melanie Yarbrough	**Interior Designer:** David Futato
	Illustrator: Rebecca Demarest

Revision History for the First Edition:
    2012-08-30   First release
See *http://oreilly.com/catalog/errata.csp?isbn=9781449324018* for release details.

ISBN: 978-1-449-32401-8

[LSI]

1346349909

Table of Contents

Preface

If you're reading this, it's because you heard about Storm somehow, and you're interested in better understanding what it does, how you can use it to solve various problems, and how it works.

This book will get you started with Storm in a very straightforward and easy way.

The first few chapters will give you a general overview of the technologies involved, some concepts you should understand so we all speak the same language, and how to install and configure Storm. The second half of the book will get you deep into spouts, bolts and topologies (more about these in a moment). The last few chapters address some more advanced features that we consider very important and interesting, like using Storm with languages that are not JVM-based.

Conventions Used in This Book

The following typographical conventions are used in this book:

Italic
: Indicates new terms, URLs, email addresses, filenames, and file extensions.

`Constant width`
: Used for program listings, as well as within paragraphs to refer to program elements such as variable or function names, databases, data types, environment variables, statements, and keywords.

`Constant width bold`
: Shows commands or other text that should be typed literally by the user.

`Constant width italic`
: Shows text that should be replaced with user-supplied values or by values determined by context.

 This icon signifies a tip, suggestion, or general note.

This icon indicates a warning or caution.

Using Code Examples

This book is here to help you get your job done. In general, you may use the code in this book in your programs and documentation. You do not need to contact us for permission unless you're reproducing a significant portion of the code. For example, writing a program that uses several chunks of code from this book does not require permission. Selling or distributing a CD-ROM of examples from O'Reilly books does require permission. Answering a question by citing this book and quoting example code does not require permission. Incorporating a significant amount of example code from this book into your product's documentation does require permission.

We appreciate, but do not require, attribution. An attribution usually includes the title, author, publisher, and ISBN. For example: "*Getting Started with Storm* by Jonathan Leibiusky, Gabriel Eisbruch, and Dario Simonassi (O'Reilly). Copyright 2012 Jonathan Leibiusky, Gabriel Eisbruch, and Dario Simonassi, 978-1-449-32401-8."

If you feel your use of code examples falls outside fair use or the permission given above, feel free to contact us at *permissions@oreilly.com*.

Safari® Books Online

 Safari Books Online (*www.safaribooksonline.com*) is an on-demand digital library that delivers expert content in both book and video form from the world's leading authors in technology and business.

Technology professionals, software developers, web designers, and business and creative professionals use Safari Books Online as their primary resource for research, problem solving, learning, and certification training.

Safari Books Online offers a range of product mixes and pricing programs for organizations, government agencies, and individuals. Subscribers have access to thousands of books, training videos, and prepublication manuscripts in one fully searchable database from publishers like O'Reilly Media, Prentice Hall Professional, Addison-Wesley Professional, Microsoft Press, Sams, Que, Peachpit Press, Focal Press, Cisco Press, John Wiley & Sons, Syngress, Morgan Kaufmann, IBM Redbooks, Packt, Adobe Press, FT Press, Apress, Manning, New Riders, McGraw-Hill, Jones & Bartlett, Course Technology, and dozens more. For more information about Safari Books Online, please visit us online.

How to Contact Us

Please address comments and questions concerning this book to the publisher:

O'Reilly Media, Inc.
1005 Gravenstein Highway North
Sebastopol, CA 95472
800-998-9938 (in the United States or Canada)
707-829-0515 (international or local)
707-829-0104 (fax)

We have a web page for this book, where we list errata, examples, and any additional information. You can access this page at *http://oreil.ly/gs_storm*.

To comment or ask technical questions about this book, send email to *bookquestions@oreilly.com*.

For more information about our books, courses, conferences, and news, see our website at *http://www.oreilly.com*.

Find us on Facebook: *http://facebook.com/oreilly*

Follow us on Twitter: *http://twitter.com/oreillymedia*

Watch us on YouTube: *http://www.youtube.com/oreillymedia*

Acknowledgements

First and foremost, we would like to thank Nathan Marz who created Storm. His effort working on this open source project is really admirable. We also would like to thank Dirk McCormick for his valuable guidance, advice, and corrections. Without his precious time spent on this book, we wouldn't have been able to finish it.

Additionally, we would like to thank Carlos Alvarez for his awesome observations and suggestions while reviewing the book.

We would like to thank Shawn Wallace from O'Reilly for guiding us through the writing and reviewing process and for providing us with a good environment and facilities to complete the project.

Also, we would like to take this opportunity to thank MercadoLibre for giving us the time to play with Storm in real-world applications. It gave us an opportunity to learn a lot about Storm.

Finally, an honorable mention goes to our families and friends for their understanding and support for us in completing this project. Without the help of the people mentioned above, we would never have made it here.

CHAPTER 1

Basics

Storm is a distributed, reliable, fault-tolerant system for processing streams of data. The work is delegated to different types of components that are each responsible for a simple specific processing task. The input stream of a Storm cluster is handled by a component called a *spout*. The spout passes the data to a component called a *bolt*, which transforms it in some way. A bolt either persists the data in some sort of storage, or passes it to some other bolt. You can imagine a Storm cluster as a chain of bolt components that each make some kind of transformation on the data exposed by the spout.

To illustrate this concept, here's a simple example. Last night I was watching the news when the announcers started talking about politicians and their positions on various topics. They kept repeating different names, and I wondered if each name was mentioned an equal number of times, or if there was a bias in the number of mentions.

Imagine the subtitles of what the announcers were saying as your input stream of data. You could have a spout that reads this input from a file (or a socket, via HTTP, or some other method). As lines of text arrive, the spout hands them to a bolt that separates lines of text into words. This stream of words is passed to another bolt that compares each word to a predefined list of politician's names. With each match, the second bolt increases a counter for that name in a database. Whenever you want to see the results, you just query that database, which is updated in real time as data arrives. The arrangement of all the components (spouts and bolts) and their connections is called a *topology* (see Figure 1-1).

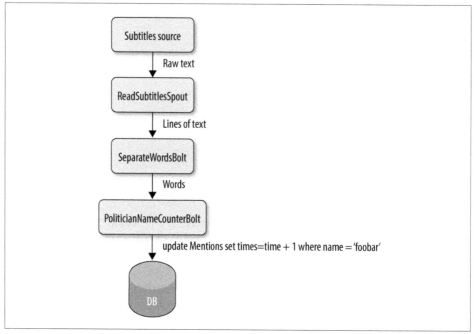

Figure 1-1. A simple topology

Now imagine easily defining the level of parallelism for each bolt and spout across the whole cluster so you can scale your topology indefinitely. Amazing, right? Although this is a simple example, you can see how powerful Storm can be.

What are some typical use cases for Storm?

Processing streams
　As demonstrated in the preceding example, unlike other stream processing systems, with Storm there's no need for intermediate queues.

Continuous computation
　Send data to clients continuously so they can update and show results in real time, such as site metrics.

Distributed remote procedure call
　Easily parallelize CPU-intensive operations.

The Components of Storm

In a Storm cluster, nodes are organized into a master node that runs continuously.

There are two kind of nodes in a Storm cluster: *master node* and *worker nodes*. Master node run a daemon called *Nimbus*, which is responsible for distributing code around the cluster, assigning tasks to each worker node, and monitoring for failures. Worker nodes run a daemon called *Supervisor*, which executes a portion of a topology. A topology in Storm runs across many worker nodes on different machines.

Since Storm keeps all cluster states either in *Zookeeper* or on local disk, the daemons are stateless and can fail or restart without affecting the health of the system (see Figure 1-2).

Figure 1-2. Components of a Storm cluster

Underneath, Storm makes use of *zeromq* (0mq, zeromq (*http://www.zeromq.org*)), an advanced, embeddable networking library that provides wonderful features that make Storm possible. Let's list some characteristics of zeromq:

- Socket library that acts as a concurrency framework
- Faster than TCP, for clustered products and supercomputing
- Carries messages across inproc, IPC, TCP, and multicast
- Asynch I/O for scalable multicore message-passing apps
- Connect N-to-N via fanout, pubsub, pipeline, request-reply

   Storm uses only push/pull sockets.

The Properties of Storm

Within all these design concepts and decisions, there are some really nice properties that make Storm unique.

Simple to program
> If you've ever tried doing real-time processing from scratch, you'll understand how painful it can become. With Storm, complexity is dramatically reduced.

Support for multiple programming languages
> It's easier to develop in a JVM-based language, but Storm supports any language as long as you use or implement a small intermediary library.

Fault-tolerant
> The Storm cluster takes care of workers going down, reassigning tasks when necessary.

Scalable

All you need to do in order to scale is add more machines to the cluster. Storm will reassign tasks to new machines as they become available.

Reliable

All messages are guaranteed to be processed at least once. If there are errors, messages might be processed more than once, but you'll never lose any message.

Fast

Speed was one of the key factors driving Storm's design.

Transactional

You can get exactly once messaging semantics for pretty much any computation.

CHAPTER 2

Getting Started

In this chapter, we'll create a Storm project and our first Storm topology.

The following assumes that you have at least version 1.6 of the Java Runtime Environment (JRE) installed. Our recommendation is to use the JRE provided by Oracle, which can be found at *http://www.java .com/downloads/*.

Operation Modes

Before we start, it's important to understand Storm *operation modes*. There are two ways to run Storm.

Local Mode

In *Local Mode*, Storm topologies run on the local machine in a single JVM. This mode is used for development, testing, and debugging because it's the easiest way to see all topology components working together. In this mode, we can adjust parameters that enable us to see how our topology runs in different Storm configuration environments. To run topologies in Local Mode, we'll need to download the Storm development dependencies, which are all the things that we need to develop and test our topologies. We'll see how soon, when we create our first Storm project.

Running a topology in Local Mode is similar to running it in a Storm cluster. However it's important to make sure that all components are *thread safe*, because when they are deployed in *Remote Mode* they may run in different JVMs or on different physical machines without direct communication or shared memory.

In all of the examples in this chapter, we'll work in Local Mode.

Remote Mode

In *Remote Mode*, we submit our topology to the Storm cluster, which is composed of many processes, usually running on different machines. Remote Mode doesn't show debugging information, which is why it's considered *Production Mode*. However, it is possible to create a Storm cluster on a single development machine, and it's a good idea to do so before deploying to production, to make sure there won't be any problems running the topology in a production environment.

You'll learn more about Remote Mode in Chapter 6, and I'll show how to install a cluster in Appendix B.

Hello World Storm

For this project, we'll create a simple topology to count words. We can consider this the "Hello World" of Storm topologies. However, it's a very powerful topology because it can scale to virtually infinite size, and with some small modifications we could even use it to create a statistical system. For example, we could modify the project to find trending topics on Twitter.

To create the topology, we'll use a spout that will be responsible for reading words, a first bolt to normalize words, and a second bolt to count words, as we can see in Figure 2-1.

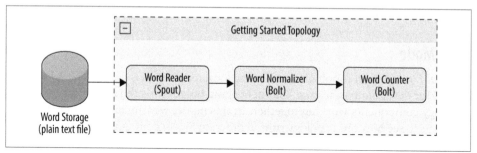

Figure 2-1. Getting started topology

You can download the source code of the example as a ZIP file at *https://github.com/storm-book/examples-ch02-getting_started/zipball/master*.

> If you use git (*http://git-scm.com/*) (a distributed revision control and source code management), you can run `git clone git@github.com:storm-book/examples-ch02-getting_started.git` into the directory where you want to download the source code.

Checking Java Installation

The first step to set up the environment is to check which version of Java you are running. Open a terminal window and run the command `java -version`. We should see something similar to the following:

```
java -version

java version "1.6.0_26"

Java(TM) SE Runtime Environment (build 1.6.0_26-b03)

Java HotSpot(TM) Server VM (build 20.1-b02, mixed mode)
```

If not, check your Java installation. (*See http://www.java.com/download/.*)

Creating the Project

To start the project, create a folder in which to place the application (as you would for any Java application). This folder will contain the project source code.

Next we need to download the Storm dependencies: a set of jars that we'll add to the application classpath. You can do so in one of two ways:

- Download the dependencies, unpack them, and add them to the classpath
- Use Apache Maven (*http://maven.apache.org/*)

> Maven is a software project management and comprehension tool. It can be used to manage several aspects of a project development cycle, from dependencies to the release build process. In this book we'll use it extensively. To check if maven is installed, run the command `mvn`. If not you can download it from *http://maven.apache.org/download.html*.
>
> Although is not necessary to be a Maven expert to use Storm, it's helpful to know the basics of how Maven works. You can find more information on the Apache Maven website (*http://maven.apache.org/*).

To define the project structure, we need to create a *pom.xml* (project object model) file, which describes dependencies, packaging, source code, and so on. We'll use the dependencies and Maven repository set up by nathanmarz (*https://github.com/nathanmarz/*). These dependencies can be found at *https://github.com/nathanmarz/storm/wiki/Maven*.

> The Storm Maven dependencies reference all the libraries required to run Storm in Local Mode.

Using these dependencies, we can write a *pom.xml* file with the basic components
necessary to run our topology:

```xml
<project xmlns="http://maven.apache.org/POM/4.0.0"
         xmlns:xsi="http://www.w3.org/2001/XMLSchema-instance"
         xsi:schemaLocation="http://maven.apache.org/POM/4.0.0
         http://maven.apache.org/xsd/maven-4.0.0.xsd">

<modelVersion>4.0.0</modelVersion>
<groupId>storm.book</groupId>
<artifactId>Getting-Started</artifactId>
<version>0.0.1-SNAPSHOT</version>

<build>
 <plugins>
   <plugin>
     <groupId>org.apache.maven.plugins</groupId>
     <artifactId>maven-compiler-plugin</artifactId>
     <version>2.3.2</version>
     <configuration>
       <source>1.6</source>
       <target>1.6</target>
       <compilerVersion>1.6</compilerVersion>
     </configuration>
   </plugin>
     </plugins>
</build>

<repositories>

    <!-- Repository where we can found the storm dependencies  -->
    <repository>
        <id>clojars.org</id>
        <url>http://clojars.org/repo</url>
    </repository>

</repositories>

<dependencies>

    <!-- Storm Dependency -->
    <dependency>
       <groupId>storm</groupId>
       <artifactId>storm</artifactId>
       <version>0.6.0</version>
    </dependency>

</dependencies>

</project>
```

The first few lines specify the project name and version. Then we add a compiler plug-
in, which tells Maven that our code should be compiled with *Java 1.6*. Next we define
the repositories (Maven supports multiple repositories for the same project). *clojars* is

the repository where Storm dependencies are located. Maven will automatically download all subdependencies required by Storm to run in Local Mode.

The application will have the following structure, typical of a Maven Java project:

```
our-application-folder/
        ├── pom.xml
        └── src
            └── main
                └── java
                │   ├── spouts
                │   └── bolts
                └── resources
```

The folders under Java will contain our source code and we'll put our Word files into the resource folder to process.

 `mkdir -p` creates all required parent directories.

Creating Our First Topology

To build our first topology, we'll create all classes required to run the word count. It's possible that some parts of the example may not be clear at this stage, but we'll explain them further in subsequent chapters.

Spout

The WordReader spout is a class that implements IRichSpout. We'll see more detail in Chapter 4. WordReader will be responsible for reading the file and providing each line to a bolt.

 A spout *emits* a list of defined fields. This architecture allows you to have different kinds of bolts reading the same spout stream, which can then define fields for other bolts to consume and so on.

Example 2-1 contains the complete code for the class (we'll analyze each part of the code following the example).

Example 2-1. src/main/java/spouts/WordReader.java

```
package spouts;

import java.io.BufferedReader;
import java.io.FileNotFoundException;
import java.io.FileReader;
```

```java
import java.util.Map;
import backtype.storm.spout.SpoutOutputCollector;
import backtype.storm.task.TopologyContext;
import backtype.storm.topology.IRichSpout;
import backtype.storm.topology.OutputFieldsDeclarer;
import backtype.storm.tuple.Fields;
import backtype.storm.tuple.Values;

public class WordReader implements IRichSpout {

        private SpoutOutputCollector collector;
        private FileReader fileReader;
        private boolean completed = false;
        private TopologyContext context;
        public boolean isDistributed() {return false;}
        public void ack(Object msgId) {
                System.out.println("OK:"+msgId);
        }
        public void close() {}
        public void fail(Object msgId) {
                System.out.println("FAIL:"+msgId);
        }

        /**
         * The only thing that the methods will do It is emit each
         * file line
         */
        public void nextTuple() {
                /**
                 * The nextuple it is called forever, so if we have been readed the file
                 * we will wait and then return
                 */
                if(completed){
                        try {
                                Thread.sleep(1000);
                        } catch (InterruptedException e) {
                                //Do nothing
                        }
                        return;
                }
                String str;
                //Open the reader
                BufferedReader reader = new BufferedReader(fileReader);
                try{
                        //Read all lines
                        while((str = reader.readLine()) != null){
                                /**
                                 * By each line emmit a new value with the line as a their
                                 */
                                this.collector.emit(new Values(str),str);
                        }
                }catch(Exception e){
                        throw new RuntimeException("Error reading tuple",e);
                }finally{
                        completed = true;
```

```
            }
    }

    /**
     * We will create the file and get the collector object
     */
    public void open(Map conf, TopologyContext context,
                        SpoutOutputCollector collector) {
            try {
                    this.context = context;
                    this.fileReader = new FileReader(conf.get("wordsFile").toString());
            } catch (FileNotFoundException e) {
                    throw new RuntimeException("Error reading file ["+conf.get("wordFile")
+"]");
            }
            this.collector = collector;
    }

    /**
     * Declare the output field "word"
     */
    public void declareOutputFields(OutputFieldsDeclarer declarer) {
            declarer.declare(new Fields("line"));
    }
}
```

The first method called in any spout is public void open(Map conf, TopologyContext context, SpoutOutputCollector collector). The parameters it receives are the TopologyContext, which contains all our topology data; the conf object, which is created in the topology definition; and the SpoutOutputCollector, which enables us to emit the data that will be processed by the bolts. The following code block is the open method implementation:

```
public void open(Map conf, TopologyContext context,
        SpoutOutputCollector collector) {
    try {
        this.context = context;
        this.fileReader = new FileReader(conf.get("wordsFile").toString());
    } catch (FileNotFoundException e) {
        throw new RuntimeException("Error reading file ["+conf.get("wordFile")+"]");
    }
    this.collector = collector;
}
```

In this method we also create the reader, which is responsible for reading the files. Next we need to implement public void nextTuple(), from which we'll emit values to be processed by the bolts. In our example, the method will read the file and emit a value per line.

```
public void nextTuple() {
    if(completed){
        try {
            Thread.sleep(1);
        } catch (InterruptedException e) {
```

```
                //Do nothing
        }
        return;
    }
    String str;
    BufferedReader reader = new BufferedReader(fileReader);
    try{
        while((str = reader.readLine()) != null){
                this.collector.emit(new Values(str));
        }
    }catch(Exception e){
        throw new RuntimeException("Error reading tuple",e);
    }finally{
        completed = true;
    }
}
```

 Values is an implementation of ArrayList, where the elements of the list are passed to the constructor.

nextTuple() is called periodically from the same loop as the ack() and fail() methods. It must release control of the thread when there is no work to do so that the other methods have a chance to be called. So the first line of nextTuple checks to see if processing has finished. If so, it should sleep for at least one millisecond to reduce load on the processor before returning. If there is work to be done, each line in the file is read into a value and emitted.

 A tuple is a named list of values, which can be of any type of Java object (as long as the object is serializable). By default, Storm can serialize common types like strings, byte arrays, ArrayList, HashMap, and Hash-Set.

Bolts

We now have a spout that reads from a file and emits one *tuple* per line. We need to create two bolts to process these tuples (see Figure 2-1). The bolts implement the backtype.storm.topology.IRichBolt interface.

The most important method in the bolt is void execute(Tuple input), which is called once per tuple received. The bolt will emit several tuples for each tuple received.

 A bolt or spout can emit as many tuples as needed. When the nextTuple or execute methods are called, they may emit 0, 1, or many tuples. You'll learn more about this in Chapter 5.

The first bolt, WordNormalizer, will be responsible for taking each line and *normalizing* it. It will split the line into words, convert all words to lowercase, and trim them.

First we need to declare the bolt's output parameters:

```
public void declareOutputFields(OutputFieldsDeclarer declarer) {
    declarer.declare(new Fields("word"));
}
```

Here we declare that the bolt will emit one Field named word.

Next we implement the public void execute(Tuple input) method, where the input tuples are processed:

```
public void execute(Tuple input) {
    String sentence = input.getString(0);
    String[] words = sentence.split(" ");
    for(String word : words){
        word = word.trim();
        if(!word.isEmpty()){
            word = word.toLowerCase();
            //Emit the word
            collector.emit(new Values(word));
        }
    }
    // Acknowledge the tuple
    collector.ack(input);
}
```

The first line reads the value from the tuple. The value can be read by position or by name. The value is processed and then emitted using the collector object. After each tuple is processed, the collector's ack() method is called to indicate that processing has completed successfully. If the tuple could not be processed, the collector's fail() method should be called.

Example 2-2 contains the complete code for the class.

Example 2-2. src/main/java/bolts/WordNormalizer.java

```
package bolts;

import java.util.ArrayList;
import java.util.List;
import java.util.Map;

import backtype.storm.task.OutputCollector;
import backtype.storm.task.TopologyContext;
import backtype.storm.topology.IRichBolt;
import backtype.storm.topology.OutputFieldsDeclarer;
import backtype.storm.tuple.Fields;
import backtype.storm.tuple.Tuple;
import backtype.storm.tuple.Values;

public class WordNormalizer implements IRichBolt {

    private OutputCollector collector;
```

```
    public void cleanup() {}

    /**
     * The bolt will receive the line from the
     * words file and process it to Normalize this line
     *
     * The normalize will be put the words in lower case
     * and split the line to get all words in this
     */
public void execute(Tuple input) {
    String sentence = input.getString(0);
    String[] words = sentence.split(" ");
    for(String word : words){
        word = word.trim();
        if(!word.isEmpty()){
            word = word.toLowerCase();
            //Emit the word
            List a = new ArrayList();
            a.add(input);
            collector.emit(a,new Values(word));
        }
    }
    // Acknowledge the tuple
    collector.ack(input);
}

    public void prepare(Map stormConf, TopologyContext context,
                    OutputCollector collector) {
        this.collector = collector;
    }

    /**
     * The bolt will only emit the field "word"
     */
    public void declareOutputFields(OutputFieldsDeclarer declarer) {
        declarer.declare(new Fields("word"));
    }

}
```

In this class, we see an example of emitting multiple tuples in a single execute call. If the method receives the sentence *This is the Storm book*, in a single **execute** call, it will emit five new tuples.

The next bolt, WordCounter, will be responsible for counting words. When the topology finishes (when the cleanup() method is called), we'll show the count for each word.

This is an example of a bolt that emits nothing. In this case, the data is added to a map, but in real life the bolt could store data to a database.

```
package bolts;

import java.util.HashMap;
import java.util.Map;
import backtype.storm.task.OutputCollector;
import backtype.storm.task.TopologyContext;
import backtype.storm.topology.IRichBolt;
import backtype.storm.topology.OutputFieldsDeclarer;
import backtype.storm.tuple.Tuple;

public class WordCounter implements IRichBolt {

        Integer id;
        String name;
        Map<String, Integer> counters;
        private OutputCollector collector;

        /**
         * At the end of the spout (when the cluster is shutdown
         * We will show the word counters
         */
        @Override
        public void cleanup() {
                System.out.println("-- Word Counter ["+name+"-"+id+"] --");
                for(Map.Entry<String, Integer> entry : counters.entrySet()){
                        System.out.println(entry.getKey()+": "+entry.getValue());
                }
        }

        /**
         * On each word We will count
         */
        @Override
        public void execute(Tuple input) {
                String str = input.getString(0);
                /**
                 * If the word dosn't exist in the map we will create
                 * this, if not We will add 1
                 */
                if(!counters.containsKey(str)){
                        counters.put(str, 1);
                }else{
                        Integer c = counters.get(str) + 1;
                        counters.put(str, c);
                }
                //Set the tuple as Acknowledge
                collector.ack(input);
        }

        /**
         * On create
         */
        @Override
        public void prepare(Map stormConf, TopologyContext context,
                        OutputCollector collector) {
```

```
                     this.counters = new HashMap<String, Integer>();
                     this.collector = collector;
                     this.name = context.getThisComponentId();
                     this.id = context.getThisTaskId();
        }

        @Override
        public void declareOutputFields(OutputFieldsDeclarer declarer) {}
    }
```

The execute method uses a *map* to collect and count the words. When the topology terminates, the cleanup() method is called and prints out the counter map. (This is just an example, but normally you should use the cleanup() method to close active connections and other resources when the topology shuts down.)

The Main Class

In the main class, you'll create the topology and a LocalCluster object, which enables you to test and debug the topology locally. In conjunction with the Config object, LocalCluster allows you to try out different cluster configurations. For example, if a global or class variable was accidentally used, you would find the error when testing your topology in configurations with a different number of workers. (You'll see more on config objects in Chapter 3.)

 All topology nodes should be able to run independently with no shared data between processes (i.e., no global or class variables) because when the topology runs in a real cluster, these processes may run on different machines.

You'll create the topology using a TopologyBuilder, which tells Storm how the nodes are arranged and how they exchange data.

```
TopologyBuilder builder = new TopologyBuilder();
builder.setSpout("word-reader",new WordReader());
builder.setBolt("word-normalizer", new WordNormalizer()).shuffleGrouping("word-
reader");
builder.setBolt("word-counter", new WordCounter()).shuffleGrouping("word-
normalizer");
```

The spout and the bolts are connected using shuffleGroupings. This type of grouping tells Storm to send messages from the source node to target nodes in randomly distributed fashion.

Next, create a `Config` object containing the topology configuration, which is merged with the cluster configuration at run time and sent to all nodes with the **prepare** method.

```
Config conf = new Config();
conf.put("wordsFile", args[0]);
conf.setDebug(true);
```

Set the property `wordsFile` to the name of the file to be read by the spout, and the property `debug` to `true` because you're in development. When debug is `true`, Storm prints all messages exchanged between nodes, and other debug data useful for understanding how the topology is running.

As explained earlier, you'll use a `LocalCluster` to run the topology. In a production environment, the topology runs continuously, but for this example you'll just run the topology for a few seconds so you can see the results.

```
LocalCluster cluster = new LocalCluster();
cluster.submitTopology("Getting-Started-Toplogie", conf, builder.createTopology());
Thread.sleep(2000);
cluster.shutdown();
```

Create and run the topology using `createTopology` and `submitTopology`, sleep for two seconds (the topology runs in a different thread), and then stop the topology by shutting down the cluster.

See Example 2-3 to put it all together.

Example 2-3. src/main/java/TopologyMain.java

```java
import spouts.WordReader;
import backtype.storm.Config;
import backtype.storm.LocalCluster;
import backtype.storm.topology.TopologyBuilder;
import backtype.storm.tuple.Fields;
import bolts.WordCounter;
import bolts.WordNormalizer;


public class TopologyMain {
    public static void main(String[] args) throws InterruptedException {

    //Topology definition
        TopologyBuilder builder = new TopologyBuilder();
        builder.setSpout("word-reader",new WordReader());
        builder.setBolt("word-normalizer", new WordNormalizer())
            .shuffleGrouping("word-reader");
        builder.setBolt("word-counter", new WordCounter(),2)
            .fieldsGrouping("word-normalizer", new Fields("word"));

    //Configuration
        Config conf = new Config();
        conf.put("wordsFile", args[0]);
        conf.setDebug(false);
    //Topology run
        conf.put(Config.TOPOLOGY_MAX_SPOUT_PENDING, 1);
```

```
        LocalCluster cluster = new LocalCluster();
        cluster.submitTopology("Getting-Started-Toplogie", conf,
            builder.createTopology());
        Thread.sleep(1000);
        cluster.shutdown();
    }
}
```

See It In Action

You're ready to run your first topology! If you create a file at src/main/resources/ words.txt with one word per line, you can run the topology with this command:

```
mvn exec:java -Dexec.mainClass="TopologyMain" -Dexec.args="src/main/resources/
words.txt"
```

For example, if you use the following *words.txt* file:

```
Storm
test
are
great
is
an
Storm
simple
application
but
very
powerful
really
Storm
is
great
```

In the logs, you should see something like the following:

```
is: 2
application: 1
but: 1
great: 1
test: 1
simple: 1
Storm: 3
really: 1
are: 1
great: 1
an: 1
powerful: 1
very: 1
```

In this example, you're only using a single instance of each node. But what if you have a very large log file? You can easily change the number of nodes in the system to parallelize the work. In this case, you'll create two instances of WordCounter:

```
builder.setBolt("word-counter", new WordCounter(),2)
        .shuffleGrouping("word-normalizer");
```

If you rerun the program, you'll see:

```
-- Word Counter [word-counter-2] --
application: 1
is: 1
great: 1
are: 1
powerful: 1
Storm: 3
-- Word Counter [word-counter-3] --
really: 1
is: 1
but: 1
great: 1
test: 1
simple: 1
an: 1
very: 1
```

Awesome! It's so easy to change the level of parallelism (in real life, of course, each instance would run on a separate machine). But there seems to be a problem: the words *is* and *great* have been counted once in each instance of WordCounter. Why? When you use shuffleGrouping, you are telling Storm to send each message to an instance of your bolt in randomly distributed fashion. In this example, it'd be ideal to always send the same word to the same WordCounter. To do so, you can change shuffleGrouping("word-normalizer") to fieldsGrouping("word-normalizer",new Fields("word")). Try it out and rerun the program to confirm the results. You'll see more about groupings and message flow in later chapters.

Conclusion

We've discussed the difference between Storm's Local and Remote operation modes, and the power and ease of development with Storm. You also learned more about some basic Storm concepts, which we'll explain in depth in the following chapters.

CHAPTER 3

Topologies

In this chapter, you'll see how to pass tuples between the different components of a Storm *topology*, and how to deploy a topology into a running Storm cluster.

Stream Grouping

One of the most important things that you need to do when designing a topology is to define how data is exchanged between components (how streams are consumed by the bolts). A *Stream Grouping* specifies which stream(s) are consumed by each `bolt` and how the stream will be consumed.

 A node can emit more than one *stream* of data. A stream grouping allows us to choose which stream to receive.

The stream grouping is set when the topology is defined, as we saw in Chapter 2:

```
...
    builder.setBolt("word-normalizer", new WordNormalizer())
        .shuffleGrouping("word-reader");
...
```

In the preceding code block, a bolt is set on the topology builder, and then a source is set using the *shuffle stream grouping*. A stream grouping normally takes the source component ID as a parameter, and optionally other parameters as well, depending on the kind of stream grouping.

 There can be more than one source per `InputDeclarer`, and each source can be grouped with a different stream grouping.

Shuffle Grouping

Shuffle Grouping is the most commonly used grouping. It takes a single parameter (the source component) and sends each tuple emitted by the source to a randomly chosen bolt warranting that each consumer will receive the same number of tuples.

The shuffle grouping is useful for doing atomic operations such as a math operation. However, if the operation can't be randomically distributed, such as the example in Chapter 2 where you needed to count words, you should consider the use of other grouping.

Fields Grouping

Fields Grouping allows you to control how tuples are sent to bolts, based on one or more fields of the tuple. It guarantees that a given set of values for a combination of fields is always sent to the same bolt. Coming back to the word count example, if you group the stream by the *word* field, the word-normalizer bolt will always send tuples with a given word to the same instance of the word-counter bolt.

```
...
builder.setBolt("word-counter", new WordCounter(),2)
    .fieldsGrouping("word-normalizer", new Fields("word"));
...
```

 All fields set in the fields grouping must exist in the sources's field declaration.

All Grouping

All Grouping sends a single copy of each tuple to all instances of the receiving bolt. This kind of grouping is used to send *signals* to bolts. For example, if you need to refresh a cache, you can send a *refresh cache signal* to all bolts. In the word-count example, you could use an all grouping to add the ability to clear the counter cache (see Topologies Example (*https://github.com/storm-book/examples-ch03-topologies*)).

```
public void execute(Tuple input) {
    String str = null;
    try{
        if(input.getSourceStreamId().equals("signals")){
            str = input.getStringByField("action");
            if("refreshCache".equals(str))
                counters.clear();
        }
    }catch (IllegalArgumentException e) {
        //Do nothing
    }
```

```
    ...
}
```

We've added an `if` to check the stream source. Storm gives us the possibility to declare named streams (if you don't send a tuple to a named stream, the stream is `"default"`); it's an excellent way to identify the source of the tuples, such as this case where we want to identify the `signals`.

In the topology definition, you'll add a second stream to the word-counter bolt that sends each tuple from the signals-spout stream to all instances of the bolt.

```
builder.setBolt("word-counter", new WordCounter(),2)
        .fieldsGrouping("word-normalizer", new Fields("word"))
        .allGrouping("signals-spout","signals");
```

The implementation of signals-spout can be found at the git repository (*https://github .com/storm-book/examples-ch03-topologies*).

Custom Grouping

You can create your own custom stream grouping by implementing the back `type.storm.grouping.CustomStreamGrouping` interface. This gives you the power to decide which bolt(s) will receive each tuple.

Let's modify the word count example, to group tuples so that all words that start with the same letter will be received by the same bolt.

```
public class ModuleGrouping implements CustomStreamGrouping, Serializable{

    int numTasks = 0;

    @Override
    public List<Integer> chooseTasks(List<Object> values) {
        List<Integer> boltIds = new ArrayList();
        if(values.size()>0){
            String str = values.get(0).toString();
            if(str.isEmpty())
                boltIds.add(0);
            else
                boltIds.add(str.charAt(0) % numTasks);
        }
        return boltIds;
    }

    @Override
    public void prepare(TopologyContext context, Fields outFields,
            List<Integer> targetTasks) {
        numTasks = targetTasks.size();
    }
}
```

You can see a simple implementation of `CustomStreamGrouping`, where we use the amount of tasks to take the modulus of the integer value of the first character of the word, thus selecting which bolt will receive the tuple.

To use this grouping in the example, change the `word-normalizer` grouping by the following:

```
builder.setBolt("word-normalizer", new WordNormalizer())
    .customGrouping("word-reader", new ModuleGrouping());
```

Direct Grouping

This is a special grouping where the source decides which component will receive the tuple. Similarly to the previous example, the source will decide which bolt receives the tuple based on the first letter of the word. To use direct grouping, in the `WordNormal izer` bolt, use the `emitDirect` method instead of `emit`.

```
public void execute(Tuple input) {
    ...
    for(String word : words){
        if(!word.isEmpty()){
            ...
            collector.emitDirect(getWordCountIndex(word),new Values(word));
        }
    }
    // Acknowledge the tuple
    collector.ack(input);
}

public Integer getWordCountIndex(String word) {
    word = word.trim().toUpperCase();
    if(word.isEmpty())
        return 0;
    else
        return word.charAt(0) % numCounterTasks;
}
```

Work out the number of target tasks in the `prepare` method:

```
public void prepare(Map stormConf, TopologyContext context,
        OutputCollector collector) {
    this.collector = collector;
    this.numCounterTasks = context.getComponentTasks("word-counter");
}
```

And in the topology definition, specify that the stream will be grouped directly:

```
builder.setBolt("word-counter", new WordCounter(),2)
    .directGrouping("word-normalizer");
```

Global Grouping

Global Grouping sends tuples generated by all instances of the source to a single target instance (specifically, the task with lowest ID).

None Grouping

At the time of this writing (Storm version 0.7.1), using this grouping is the same as using "Shuffle Grouping" on page 22. In other words, when using this grouping, it doesn't matter how streams are grouped.

LocalCluster versus StormSubmitter

Until now, you have used a utility called LocalCluster to run the topology on your local computer. Running the Storm infrastructure on your computer lets you run and debug different topologies easily. But what about when you want to submit your topology to a running Storm cluster? One of the interesting features of Storm is that it's easy to send your topology to run in a real cluster. You'll need to change the LocalCluster to a StormSubmitter and implement the submitTopology method, which is responsible for sending the topology to the cluster.

You can see the changes in the code below:

```
//LocalCluster cluster = new LocalCluster();
//cluster.submitTopology("Count-Word-Topology-With-Refresh-Cache", conf,
    builder.createTopology());
StormSubmitter.submitTopology("Count-Word-Topology-With-Refresh-Cache", conf,
    builder.createTopology());
//Thread.sleep(1000);
//cluster.shutdown();
```

 When you use a StormSubmitter, you can't control the cluster from your code as you could with a LocalCluster.

Next, package the source into a jar, which is sent when you run the Storm Client command to submit the topology. Because you used Maven, the only thing you need to do is go to the source folder and run the following:

```
mvn package
```

Once you have the generated jar, use the storm jar command to submit the topology (you should know how to install the Storm client into Appendix A). The syntax is storm jar allmycode.jar org.me.MyTopology arg1 arg2 arg3.

In this example, from the topologies source project folder, run:

```
storm jar target/Topologies-0.0.1-SNAPSHOT.jar countword.TopologyMain src/main/
resources/words.txt
```

With these commands, you have submitted the topology to the cluster.

To stop/kill it, run:

```
storm kill Count-Word-Topology-With-Refresh-Cache
```

The topology name must be unique.

To install the Storm Client, see Appendix A.

DRPC Topologies

There is a special type of topology known as *Distributed Remote Procedure Call (DRPC)*, that executes *Remote Procedure Calls (RPC)* using the distributed power of Storm (see Figure 3-1). Storm gives you some tools to enable the use of DRPC. The first is a DRPC server that runs as a connector between the client and the Storm topology, running as a source for the toplogy spouts. It receives a function to execute and its parameters. Then for each piece of data on which the function operates, the server assigns a request ID used through the topology to identify the RPC request. When the topology executes the last bolt, it must emit the RPC request ID and the result, allowing the DRPC server to return the result to the correct client.

A single DRPC server can execute many functions. Each function is identified by a unique name.

The second tool that Storm provides (used in the example) is the `LinearDRPCTopology Builder`, an abstraction to help build DRPC topologies. The topology generated creates `DRPCSpouts`—which connect to DRPC servers and emit data to the rest of the topology —and wraps bolts so that a result is returned from the last bolt. All bolts added to a `LinearDRPCTopologyBuilder` are executed in sequential order.

As an example of this type of topology, you'll create a process that adds numbers. This is a simple example, but the concept could be extended to perform complex distributed math operations.

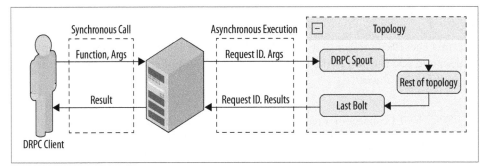

Figure 3-1. DRPC topology schema

The bolt has the following output declarer:

```
public void declareOutputFields(OutputFieldsDeclarer declarer) {
    declarer.declare(new Fields("id","result"));
}
```

Because this is the only bolt in the topology, it must emit the RPC ID and the result.

The execute method is responsible for executing the add operation:

```
public void execute(Tuple input) {
    String[] numbers = input.getString(1).split("\\+");
    Integer added = 0;
    if(numbers.length<2){
        throw new InvalidParameterException("Should be at least 2 numbers");
    }
    for(String num : numbers){
        added += Integer.parseInt(num);
    }
    collector.emit(new Values(input.getValue(0),added));
}
```

Include the added bolt in the topology definition as follows:

```
public static void main(String[] args) {
    LocalDRPC drpc = new LocalDRPC();

    LinearDRPCTopologyBuilder builder = new LinearDRPCTopologyBuilder("add");
    builder.addBolt(new AdderBolt(),2);

    Config conf = new Config();
    conf.setDebug(true);

    LocalCluster cluster = new LocalCluster();
    cluster.submitTopology("drpc-adder-topology", conf,
        builder.createLocalTopology(drpc));
    String result = drpc.execute("add", "1+-1");
    checkResult(result,0);
    result = drpc.execute("add", "1+1+5+10");
    checkResult(result,17);

    cluster.shutdown();
```

```
        drpc.shutdown();
    }
```

Create a `LocalDRPC` object that runs the DRPC server locally. Next, create a topology builder and add the bolt to the topology. To test the topology, use the **execute** method on your DRPC object.

> To connect to a remote DRPC server, use the `DRPCClient` class. The DRPC server exposes a Thrift API (*http://thrift.apache.org/*) that could be used from many languages, and it's the same API if you run DRPC server in locally or remote.
>
> To submit a topology to a Storm cluster, use the method `createRemote Topology` of the builder object instead of `createLocalTopology`, which uses the DRPC configuration from Storm config.

CHAPTER 4

Spouts

In this chapter, you'll take a look at the most commonly used strategies for designing the entry point for a topology (a spout) and how to make spouts fault-tolerant.

Reliable versus Unreliable Messages

When designing a topology, one important thing to keep in mind is message reliability. If a message can't be processed, you need to decide what to do with the individual message and what to do with the topology as a whole. For example, when processing bank deposits, it is important not to lose a single transaction message. But if you're processing millions of tweets looking for some statistical metric, and one tweet gets lost, you can assume that the metric will still be fairly accurate.

In Storm, it is the author's responsibility to guarantee message reliability according to the needs of each topology. This involves a trade-off. A reliable topology must manage lost messages, which requires more resources. A less reliable topology may lose some messages, but is less resource-intensive. Whatever the chosen reliability strategy, Storm provides the tools to implement it.

To manage reliability at the spout, you can include a message ID with the tuple at *emit* time (`collector.emit(new Values(…),tupleId)`). The methods `ack` and `fail` are called when a tuple is processed correctly or fails respectively. Tuple processing succeeds when the tuple is processed by all target bolts and all anchored bolts (you will learn how to anchor a bolt to a tuple in the Chapter 5).

Tuple processing fails when:

- `collector.fail(tuple)` is called by the target spout
- processing time exceeds the configured timeout

Let's take a look at an example. Imagine you are processing bank transactions, and you have the following requirements:

- If a transaction fails, resend the message.
- If the transaction fails too many times, terminate the topology.

You'll create a spout that sends 100 random transaction IDs, and a bolt that fails for 80% of tuples received (you can find the complete example at ch04-spout examples (*https://github.com/storm-book/examples-ch04-spouts/*)). You'll implement the spout using a Map to emit transaction message tuples so that it's easy to resend messages.

```
public void nextTuple() {
    if(!toSend.isEmpty()){
        for(Map.Entry<Integer, String> transactionEntry : toSend.entrySet()){
            Integer transactionId = transactionEntry.getKey();
            String transactionMessage = transactionEntry.getValue();
            collector.emit(new Values(transactionMessage),transactionId);
        }
        toSend.clear();
    }
}
```

If there are messages waiting to be sent, get each transaction message and its associated ID and emit them as a tuple, then clear the message queue. Note that it's safe to call clear on the map, because nextTuple, fail, and ack are the only methods that modify the map, and they all run in the same thread.

Maintain two maps to keep track of transaction messages waiting to be sent, and the number of times each transaction has failed. The ack method simply removes the transaction message from each list.

```
public void ack(Object msgId) {
    messages.remove(msgId);
    failCounterMessages.remove(msgId);
}
```

The fail method decides whether to resend a transaction message or fail if it has failed too many times.

 If you are using an all grouping in your topology and any instance of the bolt fails, the fail method of the spout will be called as well.

```
public void fail(Object msgId) {
    Integer transactionId = (Integer) msgId;
    // Check the number of times the transaction has failed
    Integer failures = transactionFailureCount.get(transactionId) + 1;

    if(fails >= MAX_FAILS){
        // If the number of failures is too high, terminate the topology
        throw new RuntimeException("Error, transaction id ["+
        transactionId+"] has had too many errors ["+failures+"]");
```

```
}

        // If the number of failures is less than the maximum, save the number and re-send
    the message
        transactionFailureCount.put(transactionId, failures);
        toSend.put(transactionId,messages.get(transactionId));
        LOG.info("Re-sending message ["+msgId+"]");
}
```

First, check the number of times the transaction has failed. If a transaction fails too many times, throw a `RuntimeException` to terminate the worker where it is running. Otherwise, save the failure count and put the transaction message in the `toSend` queue so that it will be resent when `nextTuple` is called.

 Storm nodes do not maintain state, so if you store information in memory (as in this example) and the node goes down, you will lose all stored information.

Storm is a fast-fail system. If an exception is thrown, the topology will go down, but Storm will restart the process in a consistent state so that it can recover correctly.

Getting Data

Here you'll take a look at some common techniques for designing spouts that collect data efficiently from multiple sources.

Direct Connection

In a direct connection architecture, the spout connects directly to a message emitter (see Figure 4-1).

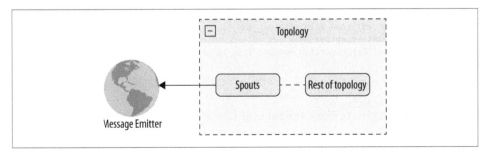

Figure 4-1. Direct connection spout

This architecture is simple to implement, particularly when the message emitter is a well-known device or a well-known device group. A well-known device is one that is known at startup and remains the same throughout the life of the topology. An unknown device is one that is added after the topology is already running. A well-known device group is one in which all devices in the group are known at start time.

As an example, create a spout to read the Twitter stream using the Twitter streaming API (*https://dev.twitter.com/docs/streaming-api*). The spout will connect directly to the API, which serves as the message emitter. Filter the stream to get all public tweets that match the **track** parameter (as documented on the Twitter dev page). The complete example can be found at Twitter Example (*https://github.com/storm-book/examples -ch04-spouts/*) github page.

The spout gets the connection parameters from the configuration object (**track**, **user**, and **password**) and creates a connection to the API (in this case, using the DefaultHttp-Client (*http://hc.apache.org/httpcomponents-client-ga/httpclient/apidocs/org/apache/ http/impl/client/DefaultHttpClient.html*) from Apache (*http://apache.org/*)). It reads the connection one line at a time, parses the line from JSON format into a Java object, and emits it.

```java
public void nextTuple() {
  //Create the client call
  client = new DefaultHttpClient();
  client.setCredentialsProvider(credentialProvider);
  HttpGet get = new HttpGet(STREAMING_API_URL+track);
  HttpResponse response;
  try {
   //Execute
   response = client.execute(get);
   StatusLine status = response.getStatusLine();
   if(status.getStatusCode() == 200){
    InputStream inputStream = response.getEntity().getContent();
    BufferedReader reader = new BufferedReader(new InputStreamReader(inputStream));
    String in;
    //Read line by line
    while((in = reader.readLine())!=null){
      try{
       //Parse and emit
       Object json = jsonParser.parse(in);
       collector.emit(new Values(track,json));
      }catch (ParseException e) {
       LOG.error("Error parsing message from twitter",e);
      }
    }
   }
  } catch (IOException e) {
    LOG.error("Error in communication with twitter api ["+get.getURI().toString()+"],
  sleeping 10s");
    try {
     Thread.sleep(10000);
    } catch (InterruptedException e1) {
    }
  }
}
```

Here you are locking the nextTuple method, so you never execute the ack and fail methods. In a real application, we recommend that you do the locking into a separate thread and use an internal queue to exchange information (you'll learn how to do that in the next example, "Enqueued Messages" on page 34).

This is great!

You're reading the Twitter stream with a single spout. If you parallelize the topology, you'll have several spouts reading different partitions of the same stream, which doesn't make sense. So how do you parallelize processing if you have several streams to read? One interesting feature of Storm is that you can access the TopologyContext from any component (spouts/bolts). Using this feature, you can divide the streams between your spout instances.

```java
public void open(Map conf, TopologyContext context,
        SpoutOutputCollector collector) {

    //Get the spout size from the context
    int spoutsSize =
context.getComponentTasks(context.getThisComponentId()).size();

    //Get the id of this spout
    int myIdx = context.getThisTaskIndex();

    String[] tracks = ((String) conf.get("track")).split(",");
    StringBuffer tracksBuffer = new StringBuffer();
    for(int i=0; i< tracks.length;i++){

        //Check if this spout must read the track word
        if( i % spoutsSize == myIdx){
            tracksBuffer.append(",");
            tracksBuffer.append(tracks[i]);
        }
    }
    if(tracksBuffer.length() == 0) {
        throw new RuntimeException("No track found for spout" +
                " [spoutsSize:"+spoutsSize+", tracks:"+tracks.length+"] the amount" +
                " of tracks must be more then the spout paralellism");
    this.track =tracksBuffer.substring(1).toString();
    }
    ...

}
```

Using this technique, you can distribute collectors evenly across data sources. The same technique can be applied in other situations—for example, for collecting log files from web servers. See Figure 4-2.

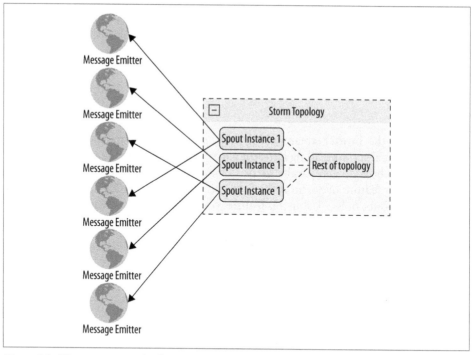

Figure 4-2. Direct connection hashing

In the previous example, you connected the spout to a well-known device. You can use the same approach to connect to unknown devices using a coordinating system to maintain the device list. The coordinator detects changes to the list and creates and destroys connections. For example, when collecting log files from web servers, the list of web servers may change over time. When a web server is added, the coordinator detects the change and creates a new spout for it. See Figure 4-3.

 It's recommended to create connections from spouts to message emitters, rather than the other way around. If the machine on which a spout is running goes down, Storm will restart it on another machine, so it's easier for the spout to locate the message emitter than for the message emitter to keep track of which machine the spout is on.

Enqueued Messages

The second approach is to connect your spouts to a *queue system* that will receive the messages from the message emitters and will leave the messages available for consumption by the spouts. The advantage of using a queue system is that it can serve as middleware between the spouts and data source; in many cases, you can use the queue to be reliable using the capability of replay messages of many queue systems. This means

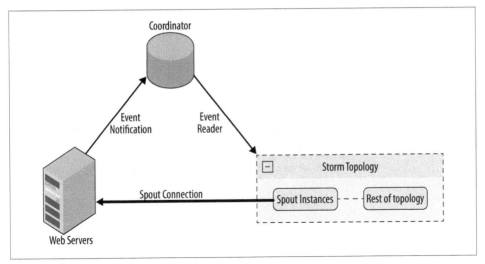

Figure 4-3. Direct connection coordinator

you don't need to know anything about message emitters, and the process of adding and removing emitters will be easier than with direct connection. The problem with this architecture is that the queue will be your point of failure, and you'll be adding a new layer to your processing flow.

Figure 4-4 shows the architecture schema.

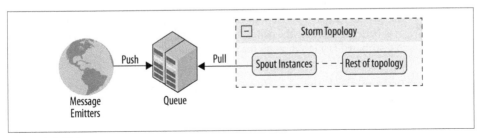

Figure 4-4. Using a queue system

 You can use round-robin pull or hashing queues (divide the queue messages by hash to send it to the spouts or create many queues) to parallelize the processing through queues, dividing the messages between many spouts.

You'll create an example using Redis (*http://redis.io*) as your queue system and their Java library, Jedis (*https://github.com/xetorthio/jedis*). In this example, you'll create a log processor to collect logs from an unknown source using the command lpush to insert messages into the queue and blpop to allow you to wait for a message. If you have many processes, using blpop will let you receive the messages in round-robin fashion.

To retrieve messages from Redis, you'll use a thread created at the open spout (using a thread to avoid locking the main loop where the nextTuple method is):

```
new Thread(new Runnable() {
    @Override
    public void run() {
        while(true){
            try{
                Jedis client = new Jedis(redisHost, redisPort);
                List<String> res = client.blpop(Integer.MAX_VALUE, queues);
                messages.offer(res.get(1));
            }catch(Exception e){
                LOG.error("Error reading queues from redis",e);
                try {
                    Thread.sleep(100);
                } catch (InterruptedException e1) {}
            }
        }
    }
}).start()
```

The only purpose of this thread is to create the connection and execute the blpop command. When a message is received, it is added to an internal queue of messages that will be consumed by the nextTuple method. Here you can see that the source is the Redis queue and you don't know which are the message emitters nor their quantity.

We recommend that you not create many threads with spout, because each spout runs in a different thread. Instead of creating many threads, it is better to increase the parallelism. This will create more threads in a distributed fashion through the Storm cluster.

In your nextTuple method, the only thing that you'll do is receive the messages and emit them again.

```
public void nextTuple() {
    while(!messages.isEmpty()){
        collector.emit(new Values(messages.poll()));
    }
}
```

You could transform this spout for the possibility of replaying messages from Redis to transform this topology into a reliable topology.

DRPC

DRPCSpout is a spout implementation that receives a function invocation stream from the DRPC server and processes it (see the example in Chapter 3). In the most common cases, using the backtype.storm.drpc.DRPCSpout (*http://nathanmarz.github.com/ storm/doc/backtype/storm/drpc/DRPCSpout.html*) will be enough, but it's possible to create your own implementation using the DRPC classes included with the Storm package.

Conclusion

You've seen the common spout implementation patterns, their advantages, and how to make the messages reliable. It's important to define spout communication based on the problem that you are working on. There is no one architecture that fits all topologies. If you know the sources or you can control these sources, then you can use a direct connection, while if you need the capacity to add unknown sources or receive messages from variety sources, it's better to use a queued connection. If you need an online process, you will need to use DRPCSpouts or implement something similar.

Although you have learned the three main types of connections, there are infinite ways to do it depending on your needs.

CHAPTER 5

Bolts

As you have seen, bolts are key components in a Storm cluster. In this chapter, you'll look at a bolt's life cycle, some strategies for bolt design, and some examples of how to implement them.

Bolt Lifecycle

A bolt is a component that takes tuples as input and produces tuples as output. When writing a bolt, you will usually implement the IRichBolt interface. Bolts are created on the client machine, serialized into the topology, and submitted to the master machine of the cluster. The cluster launches workers that deserialize the bolt, call **prepare** on it, and then start processing tuples.

 To customize a bolt, you should set parameters in its constructor and save them as instance variables so they will be serialized when submitting the bolt to the cluster.

Bolt Structure

Bolts have the following methods:

declareOutputFields(OutputFieldsDeclarer declarer)
   Declare the output schema for this bolt

prepare(java.util.Map stormConf, TopologyContext context, OutputCollector col
lector)
   Called just before the bolt starts processing tuples

execute(Tuple input)
   Process a single tuple of input

cleanup()
   Called when a bolt is going to shut down

Take a look at an example of a bolt that will split sentences into words:

```
class SplitSentence implements IRichBolt {
    private OutputCollector collector;

    public void prepare(Map conf, TopologyContext context, OutputCollector collector) {
        this.collector = collector;
    }

    public void execute(Tuple tuple) {
        String sentence = tuple.getString(0);
        for(String word: sentence.split(" ")) {
            collector.emit(new Values(word));
        }
    }

    public void cleanup() {
    }

    public void declareOutputFields(OutputFieldsDeclarer declarer) {
        declarer.declare(new Fields("word"));
    }
}
```

As you can see, this bolt is very straightforward. It's worth mentioning that in this example there is no message guarantee. This means that if the bolt discards a message for some reason—either because it goes down or because it was deliberately discarded programmatically—the spout that generated the message will never be notified, and neither will any of the bolts and spouts in between.

In many cases, you'll want to guarantee message processing through the entire topology.

Reliable versus Unreliable Bolts

As was said before, Storm guarantees that each message sent by a spout will be fully processed by all bolts. This is a design consideration, meaning that you will need to decide whether your bolts guarantee messages.

A topology is a tree of nodes in which messages (tuples) travel along one or more branches. Each node will ack(tuple) or fail(tuple) so that Storm knows when a message fails and notifies the spout or spouts that produced the message. Since a Storm topology runs in a highly parallelized environment, the best way to keep track of the original spout instance is to include a reference to the originating spout in the message tuple. This technique is called *Anchoring*. Change the SplitSentence bolt that you just saw, so that it guarantees message processing.

```
class SplitSentence implements IRichBolt {
    private OutputCollector collector;

    public void prepare(Map conf, TopologyContext context, OutputCollector collector) {
```

```
            this.collector = collector;
    }

    public void execute(Tuple tuple) {
        String sentence = tuple.getString(0);
        for(String word: sentence.split(" ")) {
            collector.emit(tuple, new Values(word));
        }
        collector.ack(tuple);
    }

    public void cleanup() {
    }

    public void declareOutputFields(OutputFieldsDeclarer declarer) {
        declarer.declare(new Fields("word"));
    }
}
```

The exact line where the anchoring happens is at the `collector.emit()` statement. As mentioned earlier, passing along the tuple enables Storm to keep track of the originating spouts. `collector.ack(tuple)` and `collector.fail(tuple)` tell a spout what happened to each message. Storm considers a tuple coming of a spout fully processed when every message in the tree has been processed. A tuple is considered failed when its tree of messages fails to be fully processed within a configurable timeout. The default is 30 seconds.

 You can change this timeout by changing the `Config.TOPOLOGY_MES` `SAGE_TIMEOUT_SECS` configuration on the topology.

Of course, the spout needs to take care of the case when a message fails and retry or discard the message accordingly.

 Every tuple you process must be acked or failed. Storm uses memory to track each tuple, so if you don't ack/fail every tuple, the task will eventually run out of memory.

Multiple Streams

A bolt can emit tuples to multiple streams using `emit(streamId, tuple)`, where `streamId` is a string that identifies the stream. Then, in the `TopologyBuilder`, you can decide which stream to subscribe to.

Multiple Anchoring

To use a bolt to join or aggregate streams, you'll need to buffer tuples in memory. In order to message guarantee in this scenario you have to anchor the stream to more than one tuple. This is done by calling emit with a List of tuples.

```
...
List<Tuple> anchors = new ArrayList<Tuple>();
anchors.add(tuple1);
anchors.add(tuple2);
_collector.emit(anchors, values);
...
```

That way, any time a bolt acks or fails, it notifies the tree, and because the stream is anchored to more than one tuple, all spouts involved are notified.

Using IBasicBolt to Ack Automatically

As you probably noticed, there are lots of use cases in which you need message guarantees. To make things easier, Storm provides another interface for bolts called IBasic Bolt, which encapsulates the pattern of calling ack right after the execute method. An implementation of this interface, BaseBasicBolt, is used to do the acking automatically.

```
class SplitSentence extends BaseBasicBolt {
    public void execute(Tuple tuple, BasicOutputCollector collector) {
        String sentence = tuple.getString(0);
        for(String word: sentence.split(" ")) {
            collector.emit(new Values(word));
        }
    }

    public void declareOutputFields(OutputFieldsDeclarer declarer) {
        declarer.declare(new Fields("word"));
    }
}
```

Tuples emitted to BasicOutputCollector are automatically anchored to the input tuple.

CHAPTER 6

A Real-Life Example

The idea of this chapter is to illustrate a typical web analytics solution, a problem that is often solved using a Hadoop batch job. Unlike a Hadoop implementation, a Storm-based solution will show results that are refreshed in *real time*.

Our example has three main components (see Figure 6-1):

- A Node.js web application, to test the system
- A Redis server, to persist the data
- A Storm topology, for real-time distributed data processing

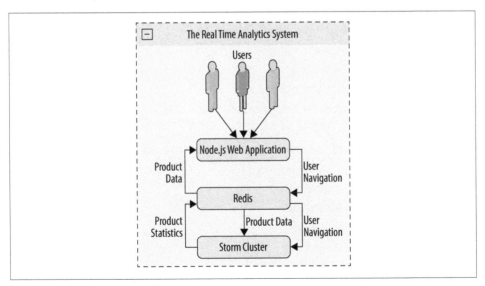

Figure 6-1. Architecture overview

If you want to go through this chapter while playing with the example, you should first read Appendix C.

The Node.js Web Application

We have mocked up a simple e-commerce website with three pages: a home page, a product page, and a product statistics page. This application is implemented using the Express Framework (*http://expressjs.com/*) and Socket.io Framework (*http://socket.io/*) to push updates to the browser. The idea of the application is to let you play with the cluster and see the results, but it's not the focus of this book, so we won't go into any more detail than a description of the pages it has.

The Home Page

This page provides links to all the products available on the platform to ease navigation between them. It lists all the items and reads them from the Redis Server. The URL for this page is *http://localhost:3000/*. (See Figure 6-2.)

Available Products:

Dvd player with surround sound system

Full HD Bluray and DVD player

Media player with USB 2.0 input

Full HD Camera

Waterproof HD Camera

ShockProof and Waterproof HD Camera

Reflex Camera

DualCore Android Smartphon with 64Gb SD card

Regular Movile Phone

Satellite phone

64Gb SD Card

32Gb SD Card

16Gb SD Card

Pink smartphone cover

Black smartphone cover

Kids smartphone cover

Figure 6-2. Home page

The Product Page

The Product Page shows information related to a specific product, such as price, title, and category. The URL for this page is *http://localhost:3000/product/:id*. (See Figure 6-3.)

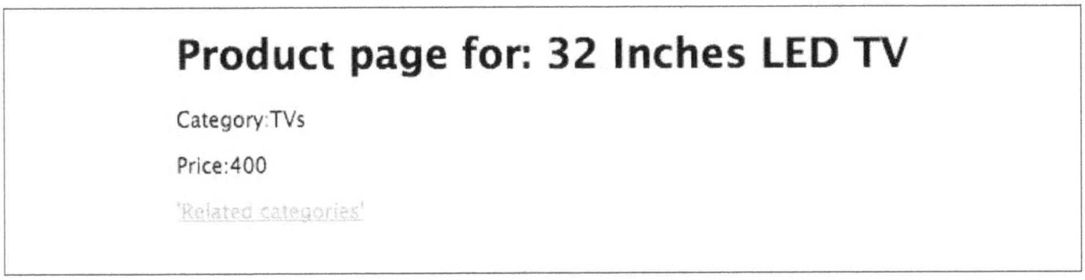

Product page for: 32 Inches LED TV

Category:TVs

Price:400

'Related categories'

Figure 6-3. Product page

The Product Stats Page

This page shows the information computed by the Storm cluster, which is collected as users navigate the website. It can be summarized as follows: users that viewed this *Product* looked at Products in those *Categories* n times. The URL for this page is *http://localhost:3000/product/:id/stats*. (See Figure 6-4.)

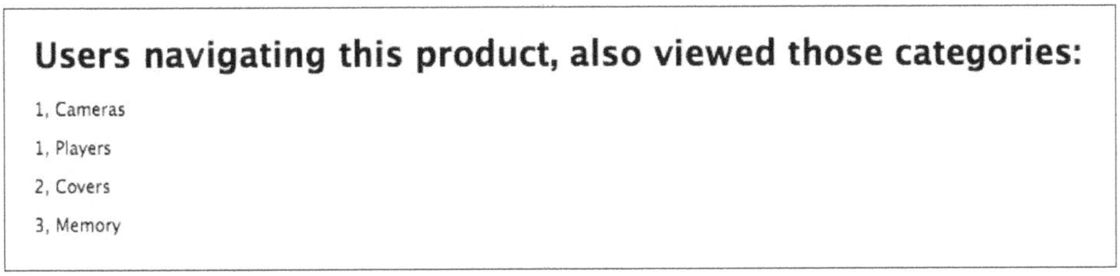

Users navigating this product, also viewed those categories:

1, Cameras

1, Players

2, Covers

3, Memory

Figure 6-4. Product stats view

Starting the Node.js Web Application

After starting the Redis server, start the web application by running the following command on the project's path:

```
node webapp/app.js
```

The web application will automatically populate Redis with some sample products for you to play with.

The Storm Topology

The goal of the Storm topology in this system is to update the product stats in real time while users navigate the website. The *Product Stats Page* is shows a list of categories with an associated counter, showing the number of users that visited other products in the same category. This helps sellers to understand their customers' needs. The topology receives a navigation log and updates the product stats as shown in the Figure 6-5.

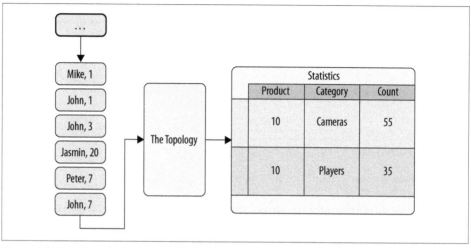

Figure 6-5. Storm topology inputs and outputs

Our Storm Topology has five components: one spout to feed it and four bolts to get the job done.

UsersNavigationSpout
> Reads from the users navigation queue and feeds the topology

GetCategoryBolt
> Reads the product information from the Redis Server and adds its category to the stream

UserHistoryBolt
> Reads the products previously navigated by the user and emits Product:Category pairs to update the counters in the next step

ProductCategoriesCounterBolt
> Keeps track of the number of times that users viewed a product of a specific category

NewsNotifierBolt
> Tells the web application to update the user interface immediately

Here's how the topology is created (see Figure 6-6):

```
package storm.analytics;
...
public class TopologyStarter {
    public static void main(String[] args) {
        Logger.getRootLogger().removeAllAppenders();

        TopologyBuilder builder = new TopologyBuilder();
```

```
    builder.setSpout("read-feed", new UsersNavigationSpout(), 3);

    builder.setBolt("get-categ", new GetCategoryBolt(), 3)
               .shuffleGrouping("read-feed");

    builder.setBolt("user-history", new UserHistoryBolt(), 5)
            .fieldsGrouping("get-categ", new Fields("user"));

    builder.setBolt("product-categ-counter", new ProductCategoriesCounterBolt(), 5)
               .fieldsGrouping("user-history", new Fields("product"));

    builder.setBolt("news-notifier", new NewsNotifierBolt(), 5)
               .shuffleGrouping("product-categ-counter");

    Config conf = new Config();
    conf.setDebug(true);

    conf.put("redis-host", REDIS_HOST);
    conf.put("redis-port", REDIS_PORT);
    conf.put("webserver", WEBSERVER);

    LocalCluster cluster = new LocalCluster();
    cluster.submitTopology("analytics", conf, builder.createTopology());
  }
}
```

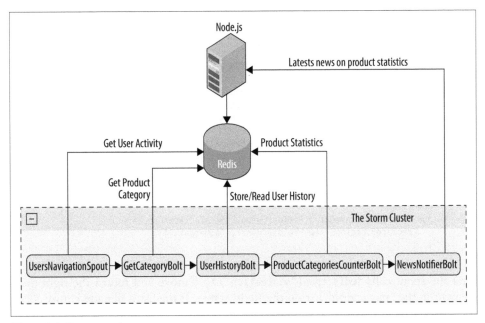

Figure 6-6. Storm topology

UsersNavigationSpout

The `UsersNavigationSpout` is in charge of feeding the topology with navigation entries. Each navigation entry is a reference to a product page viewed by one user. They are stored in the Redis Server by the web application. We'll go into more detail on that in a moment.

To read entries from the Redis server, you'll be using *https://github.com/xetorthio/jedis*, a blazingly small and simple Redis client for Java.

 Only the relevant part of the code is shown in the following code block.

```
package storm.analytics;

public class UsersNavigationSpout extends BaseRichSpout {
    Jedis jedis;

    ...

    @Override
    public void nextTuple() {
        String content = jedis.rpop("navigation");
        if(content==null || "nil".equals(content)) {
            try { Thread.sleep(300); } catch (InterruptedException e) {}
        } else {
            JSONObject obj=(JSONObject)JSONValue.parse(content);
            String user = obj.get("user").toString();
            String product = obj.get("product").toString();
            String type = obj.get("type").toString();
            HashMap<String, String> map = new HashMap<String, String>();
            map.put("product", product);
            NavigationEntry entry = new NavigationEntry(user, type, map);
            collector.emit(new Values(user, entry));
        }
    }

    @Override
    public void declareOutputFields(OutputFieldsDeclarer declarer) {
        declarer.declare(new Fields("user", "otherdata"));
    }
}
```

First the spout calls `jedis.rpop("navigation")` to remove and return the right-most element in the "navigation" list on the Redis server. If the list is already empty, sleep for 0.3 seconds so as not to block the server with a busy wait loop. If an entry is found, parse the content (the content is JSON) and map it to a `NavigationEntry` object, which is just a POJO containing the entry information:

- The user that was navigating.
- The type of page that the user browsed.
- Additional page information that depends on the type. The "PRODUCT" page type has an entry for the product ID being browsed.

The spout emits a tuple containing this information by calling `collector.emit(new Values(user, entry))`. The content of this tuple is the input to the next bolt in the topology: The GetCategoryBolt.

GetCategoryBolt

This is a very simple bolt. Its sole responsibility is to deserialize the content of the tuple emitted by the previous spout. If the entry is about a product page, then it loads the product information from the Redis server by using the ProductsReader helper class. Then, for each tuple in the input, it emits a new tuple with further product specific information:

- The user
- The product
- The category of the product

```
package storm.analytics;

public class GetCategoryBolt extends BaseBasicBolt {
    private ProductsReader reader;

    ...
    @Override
    public void execute(Tuple input, BasicOutputCollector collector) {
        NavigationEntry entry = (NavigationEntry)input.getValue(1);
        if("PRODUCT".equals(entry.getPageType())){
            try {
                String product = (String)entry.getOtherData().get("product");

                // Call the items API to get item information
                Product itm = reader.readItem(product);
                if(itm ==null)
                    return ;

                String categ = itm.getCategory();

                collector.emit(new Values(entry.getUserId(), product, categ));

            } catch (Exception ex) {
                System.err.println("Error processing PRODUCT tuple"+ ex);
                ex.printStackTrace();
            }
        }
    }
}
```

```
        ...
    }
```

As mentioned earlier, use the ProductsReader helper class to read the product specific information.

```
package storm.analytics.utilities;
...
public class ProductsReader {
    ...
    public Product readItem(String id) throws Exception{
        String content= jedis.get(id);
        if(content == null  || ("nil".equals(content)))
            return null;
        Object obj=JSONValue.parse(content);
        JSONObject product=(JSONObject)obj;
        Product i= new Product((Long)product.get("id"),
                               (String)product.get("title"),
                               (Long)product.get("price"),
                               (String)product.get("category"));
        return i;
    }
    ...
}
```

UserHistoryBolt

The UserHistoryBolt is the core of the application. It's responsible for keeping track of the products navigated by each user and determining the result pairs that should be incremented.

You'll use the Redis server to store product history by user, and you'll also keep a local copy for performance reasons. You hid the data access details in the methods getUser NavigationHistory(*user*) and addProductToHistory(*user*,*prodKey*) for read and write access, respectively.

```
package storm.analytics;
...
public class UserHistoryBolt extends BaseRichBolt{
    @Override
    public void execute(Tuple input) {
        String user = input.getString(0);
        String prod1 = input.getString(1);
        String cat1 = input.getString(2);

        // Product key will have category information embedded.
        String prodKey = prod1+":"+cat1;

        Set<String> productsNavigated = getUserNavigationHistory(user);

        // If the user previously navigated this item -> ignore it
        if(!productsNavigated.contains(prodKey)) {

            // Otherwise update related items
```

```
            for (String other : productsNavigated) {
                String [] ot = other.split(":");
                String prod2 = ot[0];
                String cat2 = ot[1];
                collector.emit(new Values(prod1, cat2));
                collector.emit(new Values(prod2, cat1));
            }
            addProductToHistory(user, prodKey);
        }
    }
}
```

Note that the desired output of this bolt is to emit the products whose categories rela-
tions should be incremented.

Take a look at the source code. The bolt keeps a *set* of the products navigated by each
user. Note that the set contains product:category pairs rather than just products. That's
because you'll need the category information in future calls and it will perform better
if you don't need to get them from the database each time. This is possible because the
products have only one category, and it won't change during the product's lifetime.

After reading the set of the user's previously navigated products (with their categories),
check if the current product has been visited previously. If so, the entry is ignored. If
this is the first time the user has visited this product, iterate through the user's history
and emit a tuple for the product being navigated and the categories of all the products
in the history with collector.emit(new Values(prod1, cat2)), and a second tuple for
the other products and the category of the product being navigated with collec
tor.emit(new Values(prod2, cat1)). Finally, add the product and its category to the set.

For example, assume that the user John has the following navigation history:

User	#	Category
John	0	Players
John	2	Players
John	17	TVs
John	21	Mounts

And the following navigation entry needs to be processed:

User	#	Category
John	8	Phones

The user hasn't yet looked at product 8, so you need to process it.

Therefore the emited tuples will be:

#	Category
8	Players
8	Players
8	TVs
8	Mounts
0	Phones
2	Phones
17	Phones
21	Phones

Note that the relation between the products on the left and the categories on the right should be incremented in one unit.

Now, let's explore the persistence used by the Bolt.

```
public class UserHistoryBolt extends BaseRichBolt{
    ...
    private Set<String> getUserNavigationHistory(String user) {
        Set<String> userHistory = usersNavigatedItems.get(user);
        if(userHistory == null) {
            userHistory = jedis.smembers(buildKey(user));
            if(userHistory == null)
                userHistory = new HashSet<String>();
            usersNavigatedItems.put(user, userHistory);
        }
        return userHistory;
    }

    private void addProductToHistory(String user, String product) {
        Set<String> userHistory = getUserNavigationHistory(user);
        userHistory.add(product);
        jedis.sadd(buildKey(user), product);
    }
    ...
}
```

The getUserNavigationHistory method returns the set of products that the user has visited. First, attempt to get the user's history from local memory with usersNavigatedItems.get(user), but if it's not there, read from the Redis server using jedis.smembers(buildKey(user)) and add the entry to the memory structure usersNavigatedItems.

When the user navigates to a new product, call addProductToHistory to update both the memory structure with userHistory.add(product) and the Redis server structure with jedis.sadd(buildKey(user), product).

Note that as long as the bolt keeps information in memory by user, it's very important that when you parallelize it you use fieldsGrouping by user in the first degree, otherwise different copies of the user history will get out of synch.

ProductCategoriesCounterBolt

The ProductCategoriesCounterBolt class is in charge of keeping track of all the product-category relationships. It receives the product-category pairs emitted by the UsersHistoryBolt and updates the counters.

The information about the number of occurrences of each pair is stored on the Redis server. A local cache for reads and a write buffer are used for performance reasons. The information is sent to Redis in a background thread.

This bolt also emits a tuple with the updated counter for the input pair to feed the next bolt in the topology, the NewsNotifierBolt, which is in charge of broadcasting the news to the final users for real-time updates.

```
public class ProductCategoriesCounterBolt extends BaseRichBolt {
    ...
    @Override
    public void execute(Tuple input) {
        String product = input.getString(0);
        String categ = input.getString(1);
        int total = count(product, categ);
        collector.emit(new Values(product, categ, total));
    }
    ...
    private int count(String product, String categ) {
        int count = getProductCategoryCount(categ, product);
        count ++;
        storeProductCategoryCount(categ, product, count);
        return count;
    }
    ...
}
```

Persistence in this bolt is hidden in the getProductCategoryCount and storeProductCategoryCount methods. Let's take a look inside them:

```
package storm.analytics;
...
public class ProductCategoriesCounterBolt extends BaseRichBolt {
    // ITEM:CATEGORY -> COUNT
    HashMap<String, Integer> counter = new HashMap<String, Integer>();

    // ITEM:CATEGORY -> COUNT
    HashMap<String, Integer> pendingToSave = new HashMap<String, Integer>();

    ...
    public int getProductCategoryCount(String categ, String product) {
        Integer count = counter.get(buildLocalKey(categ, product));
        if(count == null) {
```

```
                String sCount = jedis.hget(buildRedisKey(product), categ);
                if(sCount == null || "nil".equals(sCount)) {
                    count = 0;
                } else {
                    count = Integer.valueOf(sCount);
                }
            }
            return count;
        }
        ...
        private void storeProductCategoryCount(String categ, String product, int count) {
            String key = buildLocalKey(categ, product);
            counter.put(key , count);
            synchronized (pendingToSave) {
                pendingToSave.put(key, count);
            }
        }
        ...
    }
```

The getProductCategoryCount method first looks in memory cache counter. If the information is not available there, it gets it from the Redis server.

The storeProductCategoryCount method updates the counter cache and the pendingToSave buffer. The buffer is persisted by the following background thread:

```
package storm.analytics;

public class ProductCategoriesCounterBolt extends BaseRichBolt {
...
    private void startDownloaderThread() {
        TimerTask t = new TimerTask() {
            @Override
            public void run() {
                HashMap<String, Integer> pendings;
                synchronized (pendingToSave) {
                    pendings = pendingToSave;
                    pendingToSave = new HashMap<String, Integer>();
                }

                for (String key : pendings.keySet()) {
                    String[] keys = key.split(":");
                    String product = keys[0];
                    String categ = keys[1];
                    Integer count = pendings.get(key);
                    jedis.hset(buildRedisKey(product), categ, count.toString());
                }
            }
        };
        timer = new Timer("Item categories downloader");
        timer.scheduleAtFixedRate(t, downloadTime, downloadTime);
    }
...
}
```

The download thread locks pendingToSave, and creates a new empty buffer for the other threads to use while it sends the old one to Redis. This code block runs each downloadTime milliseconds and is configurable through the download-time topology configuration parameter. The longer the download-time is, the fewer writes to Redis are performed because consecutive adds to a pair are written just once.

Keep in mind that again, as in the previous bolt, it is extremely important to apply the correct fields grouping when assigning sources to this bolt, in this case grouping by product. That's because it stores in-memory copies of the information by product, and if several copies of the cache and the buffer exist there will be inconsistencies.

NewsNotifierBolt

The NewsNotifierBolt is in charge of notifying the web application of changes in the statistics, in order for users to be able to view changes in real time. The notification is made by HTTP POST using Apache HttpClient (*http://hc.apache.org/httpcomponents -client-ga/httpclient/index.html*), to the URL configured in the web server parameter of the topology configuration. The POST body is encoded in JSON.

This bolt is removed from the topology when testing.

```
package storm.analytics;
...
public class NewsNotifierBolt extends BaseRichBolt {
    ...
    @Override
    public void execute(Tuple input) {
        String product = input.getString(0);
        String categ = input.getString(1);
        int visits = input.getInteger(2);

        String content = "{ \"product\": \""+product+"\", \"categ\":\""+categ+"\",
\"visits\":"+visits+" }";

        HttpPost post = new HttpPost(webserver);
        try {
            post.setEntity(new StringEntity(content));
            HttpResponse response = client.execute(post);
            org.apache.http.util.EntityUtils.consume(response.getEntity());
        } catch (Exception e) {
            e.printStackTrace();
            reconnect();
        }
    }
    ...
}
```

The Redis Server

Redis is an advanced in-memory Key Value Store with support for persistence (see http://redis.io (*http://redis.io/*)). Use it to store the following information:

- The product information, used to serve the website.
- The User Navigation Queue, used to feed the Storm Topology.
- The Storm Topology Intermediate Data, used by the Topology to recover from failures.
- The Storm Topology Results, used to store the desired results.

Product Information

The Redis Server stores the products using the product ID for the key and a JSON object containing all the product information as the value.

```
> redis-cli
redis 127.0.0.1:6379> get 15
"{\"title\":\"Kids smartphone cover\",\"category\":\"Covers\",\"price\":30,\"id\":
15}"
```

User Navigation Queue

The user navigation queue is stored in a Redis list named navigation and organized as a first-in-first-out (FIFO) queue. The server adds an entry to the left side of the list each time a user visits a product page, indicating which user viewed which product. The storm cluster constantly removes elements from the right side of the list to process the information.

```
redis 127.0.0.1:6379> llen navigation
(integer) 5
redis 127.0.0.1:6379> lrange navigation 0 4
1) "{\"user\":\"59c34159-0ecb-4ef3-a56b-99150346f8d5\",\"product\":\"1\",\"type\":
\"PRODUCT\"}"
2) "{\"user\":\"59c34159-0ecb-4ef3-a56b-99150346f8d5\",\"product\":\"1\",\"type\":
\"PRODUCT\"}"
3) "{\"user\":\"59c34159-0ecb-4ef3-a56b-99150346f8d5\",\"product\":\"2\",\"type\":
\"PRODUCT\"}"
4) "{\"user\":\"59c34159-0ecb-4ef3-a56b-99150346f8d5\",\"product\":\"3\",\"type\":
\"PRODUCT\"}"
5) "{\"user\":\"59c34159-0ecb-4ef3-a56b-99150346f8d5\",\"product\":\"5\",\"type\":
\"PRODUCT\"}"
```

Intermediate Data

The cluster needs to store the history of each user separately. In order to do so, it saves a set in the Redis server with all the products and their categories that were navigated by each user.

```
redis 127.0.0.1:6379> smembers history:59c34159-0ecb-4ef3-a56b-99150346f8d5
1) "1:Players"
2) "5:Cameras"
3) "2:Players"
4) "3:Cameras"
```

Results

The cluster generates useful data about the customers viewing a specific product and stores them in a Redis Hash named "prodcnt:" followed by the product ID.

```
redis 127.0.0.1:6379> hgetall prodcnt:2
1) "Players"
2) "1"
3) "Cameras"
4) "2"
```

Testing the Topology

In order to test the topology, use the provided LocalCluster and a local Redis server (see Figure 6-7). You'll populate the products database on init and mock the insertion of navigation logs in the Redis server. Our assertions will be performed by reading the topology outputs to the Redis server. Tests are written in Java and Groovy.

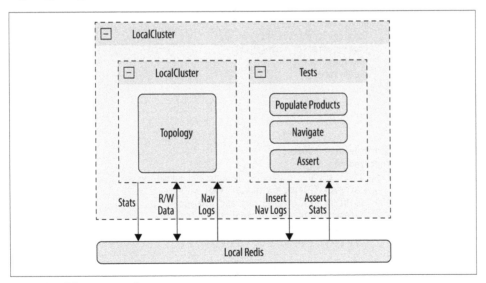

Figure 6-7. The testing architecture

Test Initialization

Initialization consists of three steps:

Start the LocalCluster and submit the Topology. Initialization is implemented in the AbstractAnalyticsTest, which is extended by all tests. A static flag called topologyStarted is used to avoid initializing more than once when multiple AbstractAnalyticsTest subclasses are instantiated.

Note that the sleep is there to allow the LocalCluster to start correctly before attempting to retrieve results from it.

```
public abstract class AbstractAnalyticsTest extends Assert {
    def jedis
    static topologyStarted = false
    static sync= new Object()

    private void reconnect() {
        jedis = new Jedis(TopologyStarter.REDIS_HOST, TopologyStarter.REDIS_PORT)
    }

    @Before
    public void startTopology(){
        synchronized(sync){
            reconnect()
            if(!topologyStarted){
                jedis.flushAll()
                populateProducts()
                TopologyStarter.testing = true
                TopologyStarter.main(null)
                topologyStarted = true
                sleep 1000
            }
        }
    }
}

...
public void populateProducts() {
    def testProducts = [
        [id: 0, title:"Dvd player with surround sound system",
            category:"Players", price: 100],
        [id: 1, title:"Full HD Bluray and DVD player",
            category:"Players", price:130],
        [id: 2, title:"Media player with USB 2.0 input",
            category:"Players", price:70],
        ...
        [id: 21, title:"TV Wall mount bracket 50-55 Inches",
            category:"Mounts", price:80]
    ]

    testProducts.each() { product ->
        def val =
"{ \"title\": \"${product.title}\" , \"category\": \"${product.category}\"," +
" \"price\": ${product.price}, \"id\": ${product.id} }"
        println val
```

```
                jedis.set(product.id.toString(), val.toString())
            }
        }
        ...
    }
```

Implement a method called navigate in the AbstractAnalyticsTest class. In order for the different tests to have a way to emulate the behavior of a user navigating the website, this step inserts navigation entries in the Redis server navigation queue.

```
    public abstract class AbstractAnalyticsTest extends Assert {
        ...
        public void navigate(user, product) {
            String nav =
     "{\"user\": \"${user}\", \"product\": \"${product}\", \"type\": \"PRODUCT
     \"}".toString()
            println "Pushing navigation: ${nav}"
            jedis.lpush('navigation', nav)
        }
        ...
    }
```

Provide a method called getProductCategoryStats in the AbstractAnalyticsTest that reads a specific relation from the Redis server. Different tests will also need to assert against the statistics results in order to check if the topology is behaving as expected.

```
    public abstract class AbstractAnalyticsTest extends Assert {
        ...
        public int getProductCategoryStats(String product, String categ) {
            String count = jedis.hget("prodcnt:${product}", categ)
            if(count == null || "nil".equals(count))
                return 0
            return Integer.valueOf(count)
        }
        ...
    }
```

A Test Example

In the next snippet, you'll emulate a few product navigations of user "1", then check the results. Note that you wait two seconds before asserting to be sure that the results have been stored to Redis. (Remember that the ProductCategoriesCounterBolt has an in-memory copy of the counters and sends them to Redis in the background.)

```
    package functional

    class StatsTest extends AbstractAnalyticsTest {
        @Test
        public void testNoDuplication(){
            navigate("1", "0") // Players
            navigate("1", "1") // Players
            navigate("1", "2") // Players
            navigate("1", "3") // Cameras
```

```
Thread.sleep(2000) // Give two seconds for the system to process the data.

        assertEquals 1, getProductCategoryStats("0", "Cameras")
        assertEquals 1, getProductCategoryStats("1", "Cameras")
        assertEquals 1, getProductCategoryStats("2", "Cameras")
        assertEquals 2, getProductCategoryStats("0", "Players")
        assertEquals 3, getProductCategoryStats("3", "Players")
    }
}
```

Notes on Scalability and Availability

The architecture of this solution has been simplified to fit into a single chapter of the book. For that reason, you avoided some complexity that would be necessary for this solution to scale and have high availability. There are a couple of major issues with this approach.

The Redis server in this architecture is not only a *single point of failure* but also a bottleneck. You'll be able to receive only as much traffic as the Redis server can handle. The Redis layer can be scaled by using sharding, and its availability can be improved by using a Master/Slave configuration, which would require changes to the sources of both the topology and the web application.

Another weakness is that the web application does not scale proportionately by adding servers in a round robin fashion. This is because it needs to be notified when some product statistic changes and to notify all interested browsers. This "notification to browser" bridge is implemented using Socket.io, but it requires that the listener and the notifier be hosted on the same web server. This is achievable only if you shard the GET /product/:id/stats traffic and the POST /news traffic, both with same criteria, ensuring that requests referencing the same product will end up on the same server.

CHAPTER 7

Using Non-JVM Languages with Storm

Sometimes you want to use languages that aren't based on the JVM to implement a Storm project, either because you feel more comfortable with another language or you want to use a library written in that language.

Storm is implemented in Java, and all the spouts and bolts that you've seen in this book were written in Java as well. So is it possible to use languages like Python, Ruby, or even JavaScript to write spouts and bolts? The answer is yes! It is possible using something called the *multilang protocol*.

The multilang protocol is a special protocol implemented in Storm that uses *standard input* and *standard output* as a channel of communication with a process that does the job of a spout or a bolt. Messages are passed through this channel encoded as JSON or as lines of plain text.

Let's take a look at a simple example of a spout and a bolt in a non-JVM language. You'll have a spout that generates numbers from 1 to 10,000 and a bolt that filters for prime numbers, both written in PHP.

 In this example, we check for prime numbers in a naive way. There are much better implementations, but they are also more complex and out of the scope of this example.

There is an official implementation of a PHP DSL for Storm. In this chapter, we'll show our implementation as an example. First of all, define the topology.

```
...
TopologyBuilder builder = new TopologyBuilder();
builder.setSpout("numbers-generator", new NumberGeneratorSpout(1, 10000));
builder.setBolt("prime-numbers-filter", new
PrimeNumbersFilterBolt()).shuffleGrouping("numbers-generator");
StormTopology topology = builder.createTopology();
...
```

There is a way to specify topologies in a non-JVM language. Since Storm topologies are just Thrift structures, and Nimbus is a Thrift daemon, you can create and submit topologies in any language you want. But this it out of the scope of this book.

Nothing new here. Let's see the implementation of NumbersGeneratorSpout.

```
public class NumberGeneratorSpout extends ShellSpout implements IRichSpout {
    public NumberGeneratorSpout(Integer from, Integer to) {
    super("php", "-f", "NumberGeneratorSpout.php", from.toString(), to
        .toString());
    }

    public void declareOutputFields(OutputFieldsDeclarer declarer) {
    declarer.declare(new Fields("number"));
    }

    public Map<String, Object> getComponentConfiguration() {
        return null;
    }
}
```

As you have probably noticed, this spout extends ShellSpout. This is a special class that comes with Storm and helps you run and control spouts written in other languages. In this case, it tells Storm how to execute your PHP script.

The NumberGeneratorSpout PHP script emits tuples to the standard output, and reads standard input to process acks or fails.

Before going over the implementation of the NumberGeneratorSpout.php script, look in more detail at how the multilang protocol works.

The spout generates sequential numbers counting from the from parameter up to the to parameter, passed to the constructor.

Next, look at PrimeNumbersFilterBolt. This class implements the shell mentioned earlier. It tells Storm how to execute your PHP script. Storm provides a special class for this purpose called ShellBolt, where the only thing you have to do is to indicate how to run the script and declare the fields that it emits.

```
public class PrimeNumbersFilterBolt extends ShellBolt implements IRichBolt {
    public PrimeNumbersFilterBolt() {
        super("php", "-f", "PrimeNumbersFilterBolt.php");
    }

    public void declareOutputFields(OutputFieldsDeclarer declarer) {
        declarer.declare(new Fields("number"));
    }
}
```

In the constructor, just tell Storm how to run the PHP script. This is the equivalent of the following bash command:

```
php -f PrimeNumbersFilterBolt.php
```

The PrimeNumbersFilterBolt PHP script reads tuples from standard input, processes them, and emits, acks, or fails to standard output. Before going over the implementation of the `PrimeNumbersFilterBolt.php` script, let's look in more detail at how the multilang protocol works.

The Multilang Protocol Specification

The protocol relies on standard input and standard output as a channel of communication between processes. Follow the steps a script needs to take in order to work:

1. Initiate a handshake.
2. Start looping.
3. Read or write tuples.

 There is a special way of logging from your script that uses Storm's built-in logging mechanism, so you don't need to implement your own logging system.

Let's take a look at the detail of each of these steps, and how to implement it using a PHP script.

Initial Handshake

In order to control the process (to start and stop it), Storm needs to know the *process ID* (PID) of the script it is executing. According to the multilang protocol, the first thing that will happen when your process starts is that Storm will send a JSON object with storm configuration, topology context, and a PID directory to standard input. It will look something like the following code block:

```
{
    "conf": {
        "topology.message.timeout.secs": 3,
        // etc
    },
    "context": {
        "task->component": {
            "1": "example-spout",
            "2": "__acker",
            "3": "example-bolt"
        },
        "taskid": 3
    },
```

```
    "pidDir": "..."
}
```

The process must create an empty file at the path specified by `pidDir`, whose name is the process ID, and write the PID to standard out as a JSON object.

```
{"pid": 1234}
```

For example, if you receive `/tmp/example\n` and the PID of your script is `123`, you should create an empty file at `/tmp/example/123` and print the lines `{"pid": 123}n` and `end\n` to standard output. This is how Storm keeps track of the PID and kills the process when it shuts down. Let's see how to do it in PHP:

```
$config = json_decode(read_msg(), true);
$heartbeatdir = $config['pidDir'];

$pid = getmypid();
fclose(fopen("$heartbeatdir/$pid", "w"));
storm_send(["pid"=>$pid]);
flush();
```

You've created a function called `read_msg` to handle reading messages from standard input. The multilang protocol states that messages can be either a single line or multiple lines encoded in JSON. A message is complete when Storm sends a single line with the word `end\n`.

```
function read_msg() {
    $msg = "";
    while(true) {
        $l = fgets(STDIN);
        $line = substr($l,0,-1);
        if($line=="end") {
            break;
        }
        $msg = "$msg$line\n";
    }
    return substr($msg, 0, -1);
}

function storm_send($json) {
    write_line(json_encode($json));
    write_line("end");
}

function write_line($line) {
    echo("$line\n");
}
```

The use of `flush()` is very important; there might be a buffer that won't be flushed until a specific amount of characters are accumulated. This means that your script can hang forever waiting for an input from Storm, which it will never receive because Storm is in turn waiting on an output from your script. So it's important to make sure that when your script outputs something it gets flushed immediately.

Start Looping and Read or Write Tuples

This is the most important step, where all the work gets done. The implementation of this step depends on if you are developing a spout or a bolt.

In case of a spout, you should start emitting tuples. In case of a bolt, loop and read tuples, process them and emit, ack or fail.

Let's see the implementation of the spout that emits numbers.

```
$from = intval($argv[1]);
$to = intval($argv[2]);

while(true) {
    $msg = read_msg();

    $cmd = json_decode($msg, true);
    if ($cmd['command']=='next') {
        if ($from<$to) {
            storm_emit(array("$from"));
            $task_ids = read_msg();
            $from++;
        } else {
            sleep(1);
        }
    }
    storm_sync();
}
```

Get the from and to from the command-line arguments and start iterating. Everytime you get a next message from Storm, it means you are ready to emit a new tuple.

Once you've sent all the numbers and you don't have more tuples to send, just sleep for some time.

In order to make sure the script is ready for the next tuple, Storm waits for the line sync \n before sending the next one. To read a command, just call read_msg() and JSON decode it.

In the case of bolts, this is a little different.

```
while(true) {
    $msg = read_msg();
    $tuple = json_decode($msg, true, 512, JSON_BIGINT_AS_STRING);
    if (!empty($tuple["id"])) {
        if (isPrime($tuple["tuple"][0])) {
            storm_emit(array($tuple["tuple"][0]));
        }
        storm_ack($tuple["id"]);
    }
}
```

Loop, reading tuples from standard input. As soon as you get a message, JSON decodes it. If it is a tuple, process it, checking if it is a prime number.

In case it is a prime number, emit that number; otherwise just ignore it.

In any case, ack the tuple.

 The use of JSON_BIGINT_AS_STRING in the json_decode function is a work-around for a conversion problem between Java and PHP. Java sends some very big numbers, and they are decoded with less precision in PHP, which can cause problems. To work around this problem, tell PHP to decode big numbers as strings and to avoid using double quotes when printing numbers in JSON messages. PHP 5.4.0 or higher is required for this parameter to work.

Messages like emit, ack, fail, and log have the following structure:

Emit

```
{
    "command": "emit",
    "tuple": ["foo", "bar"]
}
```

Where the array has the values you are emitting for the tuple.

Ack

```
{
    "command": "ack",
    "id": 123456789
}
```

Where the id is the ID of the tuple you are processing.

Fail

```
{
    "command": "fail",
    "id": 123456789
}
```

Same as emit, the id is the ID of the tuple you are processing.

Log

```
{
    "command": "log",
    "msg": "some message to be logged by storm."
}
```

Putting it all together gives you the following PHP scripts.

For your spout:

```php
<?php
function read_msg() {
    $msg = "";
    while(true) {
        $l = fgets(STDIN);
        $line = substr($l,0,-1);
        if ($line=="end") {
            break;
        }
        $msg = "$msg$line\n";
    }
    return substr($msg, 0, -1);
}

function write_line($line) {
    echo("$line\n");
}

function storm_emit($tuple) {
    $msg = array("command" => "emit", "tuple" => $tuple);
    storm_send($msg);
}

function storm_send($json) {
    write_line(json_encode($json));
    write_line("end");
}

function storm_sync() {
    storm_send(array("command" => "sync"));
}

function storm_log($msg) {
    $msg = array("command" => "log", "msg" => $msg);
    storm_send($msg);
    flush();
}

$config = json_decode(read_msg(), true);
$heartbeatdir = $config['pidDir'];

$pid = getmypid();
fclose(fopen("$heartbeatdir/$pid", "w"));
storm_send(["pid"=>$pid]);
flush();

$from = intval($argv[1]);
$to = intval($argv[2]);

while(true) {
    $msg = read_msg();

    $cmd = json_decode($msg, true);
    if ($cmd['command']=='next') {
```

```php
        if ($from<$to) {
            storm_emit(array("$from"));
            $task_ids = read_msg();
            $from++;
        } else {
            sleep(1);
        }
    }
    storm_sync();
}
?>
```

And for your bolt:

```php
<?php
function isPrime($number) {
    if ($number < 2) {
        return false;
    }
    if ($number==2) {
        return true;
    }
    for ($i=2; $i<=$number-1; $i++) {
        if ($number % $i == 0) {
            return false;
        }
    }
    return true;
}
function read_msg() {
    $msg = "";
    while(true) {
        $l = fgets(STDIN);
        $line = substr($l,0,-1);
        if ($line=="end") {
            break;
        }
        $msg = "$msg$line\n";
    }
    return substr($msg, 0, -1);
}

function write_line($line) {
    echo("$line\n");
}

function storm_emit($tuple) {
    $msg = array("command" => "emit", "tuple" => $tuple);
    storm_send($msg);
}

function storm_send($json) {
    write_line(json_encode($json));
    write_line("end");
}
```

```php
function storm_ack($id) {
    storm_send(["command"=>"ack", "id"=>"$id"]);
}

function storm_log($msg) {
    $msg = array("command" => "log", "msg" => "$msg");
    storm_send($msg);
}

$config = json_decode(read_msg(), true);
$heartbeatdir = $config['pidDir'];

$pid = getmypid();
fclose(fopen("$heartbeatdir/$pid", "w"));
storm_send(["pid"=>$pid]);
flush();

while(true) {
    $msg = read_msg();
    $tuple = json_decode($msg, true, 512, JSON_BIGINT_AS_STRING);
    if (!empty($tuple["id"])) {
        if (isPrime($tuple["tuple"][0])) {
            storm_emit(array($tuple["tuple"][0]));
        }
        storm_ack($tuple["id"]);
    }
}
?>
```

 It is important to put all these scripts in a special folder called multilang/ resources in your project directory. This folder gets included in the jar file that is sent to the workers. If you don't put the scripts in that folder, Storm won't be able to run them and will report an error.

CHAPTER 8

Transactional Topologies

With Storm, you can guarantee message processing by using an ack and fail strategy, as mentioned earlier in the book. But what happens if tuples are replayed? How do you make sure you won't overcount?

Transactional Topologies is a new feature, included in Storm 0.7.0, that enables messaging semantics to ensure you replay tuples in a secure way and process them only once. Without support for transactional topologies, you wouldn't be able to count in a fully accurate, scalable, and fault-tolerant way.

 Transactional Topologies are an abstraction built on top of standard Storm spouts and bolts.

The Design

In a transactional topology, Storm uses a mix of parallel and sequential tuple processing. The spout generates batches of tuples that are processed by the bolts in parallel. Some of those bolts are known as *committers*, and they commit processed batches in a strictly ordered fashion. This means that if you have two batches with five tuples each, both tuples will be processed in parallel by the bolts, but the committer bolts won't commit the second tuple until the first tuple is committed successfully.

 When dealing with transactional topologies, it is important to be able to replay batch of tuples from the source, and sometimes even several times. So make sure your source of data—the one that your spout will be connected to—has the ability to do that.

This can be described as two different steps, or phases:

The processing phase
   A fully parallel phase, many batches are executed at the same time.

The commit phase
   A strongly ordered phase, batch two is not committed until batch one has committed successfully.

Call both of these phases a *Storm Transaction.*

 Storm uses Zookeeper to store transaction metadata. By default the one used for the topology, will be used to store the metadata. You can change this by overriding the configuration key *transactional.zookeeper.servers* and *transactional.zookeeper.port.*

Transactions in Action

To see how transactions work, you'll create a Twitter analytics tool. You'll be reading tweets stored in a Redis database, process them through a few bolts, and store—in another Redis database—the list of all hashtags and their frequency among the tweets, the list of all users and amount of tweets they appear in, and a list of users with their hashtags and frequency.

The topology you'll build for this tool is described in Figure 8-1.

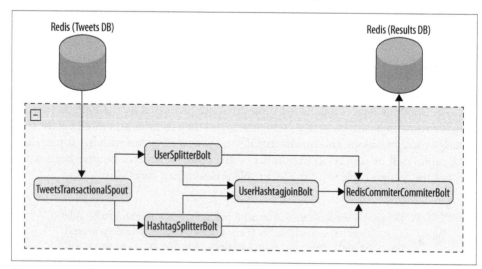

Figure 8-1. Topology overview

As you can see, TweetsTransactionalSpout is the spout that will be connecting to your tweets database and will be emitting batches of tuples across the topology. Two different bolts, `UserSplitterBolt` and `HashtagSplitterBolt`, will receive tuples from the spout. `UserSplitterBolt` will parse the tweet and look for users—words preceded by @—and will emit these words in a custom stream called *users*. The `HashatagSplitter Bolt` will also parse the tweet, looking for words preceded by #, and will emit these words in a custom stream called *hashtags*. A third bolt, the `UserHashtagJoinBolt`, will receive both streams and count how many times a hashtag has appeared in a tweet where a user was named. In order to count and emit the result, this bolt will be a `BaseBatchBolt` (more on that later).

Finally, a last bolt, called `RedisCommitterBolt`, will receive the three streams—the ones generated by `UserSplitterBolt`, `HashtagSplitterBolt`, and `UserHashtagJoinBolt`. It will count everything and once finished processing the batch of tuples, it will send everything to Redis, in one transaction. This bolt is a special kind of bolt known as a *committer bolt*, explained later in this chapter.

In order to build this topology, use `TransactionalTopologyBuilder`, like the following code block:

```
TransactionalTopologyBuilder builder =
    new TransactionalTopologyBuilder("test", "spout", new TweetsTransactionalSpout());

builder.setBolt("users-splitter", new UserSplitterBolt(), 4).shuffleGrouping("spout");
builder.setBolt("hashtag-splitter",
    new HashtagSplitterBolt(), 4).shuffleGrouping("spout");

builder.setBolt("user-hashtag-merger", new UserHashtagJoinBolt(), 4)
    .fieldsGrouping("users-splitter","users", new Fields("tweet_id"))
    .fieldsGrouping("hashtag-splitter", "hashtags", new Fields("tweet_id"));

builder.setBolt("redis-committer", new RedisCommiterCommiterBolt())
    .globalGrouping("users-splitter","users")
    .globalGrouping("hashtag-splitter", "hashtags")
    .globalGrouping("user-hashtag-merger");
```

Let's see how you can implement the spout in a transactional topology.

The Spout

The spout in a transactional topology is completely different from a standard spout.

```
public class TweetsTransactionalSpout extends
BaseTransactionalSpout<TransactionMetadata> {
```

As you can see in the class definition, `TweetsTransactionalSpout` extends `BaseTransac tionalSpout` with a generic type. The type you set there is something known as the *transaction metadata*. It will be used later to emit batches of tuples from the source.

In this example, `TransactionMetadata` is defined as:

```
public class TransactionMetadata implements Serializable {
    private static final long serialVersionUID = 1L;
```

```
    long from;
    int quantity;

    public TransactionMetadata(long from, int quantity) {
      this.from = from;
      this.quantity = quantity;
    }
  }
```

Here you'll store from and quantity, which will tell you exactly how to generate the batch of tuples.

To finish the implementation of the spout, you need to implement the following three methods:

```
@Override
public ITransactionalSpout.Coordinator<TransactionMetadata> getCoordinator(
Map conf, TopologyContext context) {
  return new TweetsTransactionalSpoutCoordinator();
}

@Override
public backtype.storm.transactional.ITransactionalSpout.Emitter<TransactionMetadata>
getEmitter(
Map conf, TopologyContext context) {
  return new TweetsTransactionalSpoutEmitter();
}

@Override
public void declareOutputFields(OutputFieldsDeclarer declarer) {
  declarer.declare(new Fields("txid", "tweet_id", "tweet"));
}
```

In the getCoordinator method, you tell Storm which class will coordinate the generation of batches of tuples. With getEmitter, you tell Storm which class will be responsible for reading batches of tuples from the source and emitting them to a stream in the topology. And finally, as you did before, you need to declare which fields are emitted.

The RQ class

To make the example easier, we've decided to encapsulate all operations with Redis in one single class.

```
public class RQ {
  public static final String NEXT_READ = "NEXT_READ";
  public static final String NEXT_WRITE = "NEXT_WRITE";

  Jedis jedis;

  public RQ() {
    jedis = new Jedis("localhost");
  }

  public long getAvailableToRead(long current) {
    return getNextWrite() - current;
```

```
      }

      public long getNextRead() {
        String sNextRead = jedis.get(NEXT_READ);
        if(sNextRead == null)
          return 1;
        return Long.valueOf(sNextRead);
      }

      public long getNextWrite() {
        return Long.valueOf(jedis.get(NEXT_WRITE));
      }

      public void close() {
        jedis.disconnect();
      }

      public void setNextRead(long nextRead) {
        jedis.set(NEXT_READ, ""+nextRead);
      }

      public List<String> getMessages(long from, int quantity) {
        String[] keys = new String[quantity];

        for (int i = 0; i < quantity; i++)
          keys[i] = ""+(i+from);

        return jedis.mget(keys);
      }
    }
```

Read carefully the implementation of each method, and make sure you understand what they do.

The Coordinator

Let's see the implementation of the coordinator of this example.

```
    public static class TweetsTransactionalSpoutCoordinator implements
    ITransactionalSpout.Coordinator<TransactionMetadata> {
      TransactionMetadata lastTransactionMetadata;
      RQ rq = new RQ();
      long nextRead = 0;

      public TweetsTransactionalSpoutCoordinator() {
        nextRead = rq.getNextRead();
      }

      @Override
      public TransactionMetadata initializeTransaction(BigInteger txid,
            TransactionMetadata prevMetadata) {
        long quantity = rq.getAvailableToRead(nextRead);
        quantity = quantity > MAX_TRANSACTION_SIZE ? MAX_TRANSACTION_SIZE : quantity;
        TransactionMetadata ret = new TransactionMetadata(nextRead, (int)quantity);
```

```
      nextRead += quantity;
      return ret;
    }

    @Override
    public boolean isReady() {
      return rq.getAvailableToRead(nextRead) > 0;
    }

    @Override
    public void close() {
      rq.close();
    }
  }
```

It is important to mention that *among the entire topology there will be only one coordinator instance*. When the coordinator is instantiated, it retrieves from Redis a sequence that tells the coordinator which is the next tweet to read. The first time, this value will be 1, which means that the next tweet to read is the first one.

The first method that will be called is `isReady`. It will always be called before `initiali zeTransaction`, to make sure the source is ready to be read from. You should return `true` or `false` accordingly. In this example, retrieve the amount of tweets and compare them with how many tweets you read. The difference between them is the amount to available tweets to read. If it is greater than 0, it means you have tweets to read.

Finally, the `initializeTransaction` is executed. As you can see, you get `txid` and `pre vMetadata` as parameters. The first one is a unique transaction ID generated by Storm, which identifies the batch of tuples to be generated. `prevMetadata` is the metadata generated by the coordinator of the previous transaction.

In this example, first make sure how many tweets are available to read. And once you have sorted that out, create a new `TransactionMetadata`, indicating which is the first tweet to read `from`, and which is the `quantity` of tweets to read.

As soon as you return the metadata, Storm stores it with the `txid` in zookeeper. This guarantees that if something goes wrong, Storm will be able to replay this with the emitter to resend the batch.

The Emitter

The final step when creating a transactional spout is implementing the emitter.

Let's start with the following implementation:

```
public static class TweetsTransactionalSpoutEmitter implements
ITransactionalSpout.Emitter<TransactionMetadata> {

  RQ rq = new RQ();

  public TweetsTransactionalSpoutEmitter() {
  }
```

```java
    @Override
    public void emitBatch(TransactionAttempt tx,
            TransactionMetadata coordinatorMeta, BatchOutputCollector collector) {
        rq.setNextRead(coordinatorMeta.from+coordinatorMeta.quantity);
        List<String> messages = rq.getMessages(coordinatorMeta.from,
            coordinatorMeta.quantity);

        long tweetId = coordinatorMeta.from;

        for (String message : messages) {
            collector.emit(new Values(tx, ""+tweetId, message));
            tweetId++;
        }
    }

    @Override
    public void cleanupBefore(BigInteger txid) {
    }

    @Override
    public void close() {
        rq.close();
    }
}
```

Emitters are the one who will read the source and send tuples to a stream. It is very important for the emitters to always be able to send the same batch of tuples for the same *transaction id* and *transaction metadata*. This way, if something goes wrong during the processing of a batch, Storm will be able to repeat the same *transaction id* and *transaction metadata* with the emitter and make sure the batch of tuples are repeated. Storm will increase the *attempt id* in the TransactionAttempt. This way you know that the batch is repeated.

The important method here is emitBatch. In this method, use the metadata, given as a parameter, to get tweets from Redis. Also increase the sequence in Redis that keeps track of how many tweets you've read so far. And of course, emit the tweets to the topology.

The Bolts

First let's see the standard bolts of this topology:

```java
public class UserSplitterBolt implements IBasicBolt{
    private static final long serialVersionUID = 1L;

    @Override
    public void declareOutputFields(OutputFieldsDeclarer declarer) {
        declarer.declareStream("users", new Fields("txid", "tweet_id", "user"));
    }

    @Override
    public Map<String, Object> getComponentConfiguration() {
        return null;
```

```
    }

    @Override
    public void prepare(Map stormConf, TopologyContext context) {
    }

    @Override
    public void execute(Tuple input, BasicOutputCollector collector) {
      String tweet = input.getStringByField("tweet");
      String tweetId = input.getStringByField("tweet_id");
      StringTokenizer strTok = new StringTokenizer(tweet, " ");
      TransactionAttempt tx = (TransactionAttempt)input.getValueByField("txid");
      HashSet<String> users = new HashSet<String>();

      while(strTok.hasMoreTokens()) {
        String user = strTok.nextToken();

        // Ensure this is an actual user, and that it's not repeated in the tweet
        if(user.startsWith("@") && !users.contains(user)) {
          collector.emit("users", new Values(tx, tweetId, user));
          users.add(user);
        }
      }
    }

    @Override
    public void cleanup() {

    }
  }
```

As mentioned earlier in this chapter, UserSplitterBolt receives tuples, parses the text of the tweet, and emits words preceded by @, or the Twitter users. HashtagSplitter Bolt works in a very similar way.

```
    public class HashtagSplitterBolt implements IBasicBolt{

      private static final long serialVersionUID = 1L;

      @Override
      public void declareOutputFields(OutputFieldsDeclarer declarer) {
        declarer.declareStream("hashtags", new Fields("txid", "tweet_id", "hashtag"));
      }

      @Override
      public Map<String, Object> getComponentConfiguration() {
        return null;
      }

      @Override
      public void prepare(Map stormConf, TopologyContext context) {
      }

      @Override
      public void execute(Tuple input, BasicOutputCollector collector) {
```

```
String tweet = input.getStringByField("tweet");
String tweetId = input.getStringByField("tweet_id");
StringTokenizer strTok = new StringTokenizer(tweet, " ");
TransactionAttempt tx = (TransactionAttempt)input.getValueByField("txid");
HashSet<String> words = new HashSet<String>();

while(strTok.hasMoreTokens()) {
  String word = strTok.nextToken();

  if(word.startsWith("#") && !words.contains(word)) {
    collector.emit("hashtags", new Values(tx, tweetId, word));
    words.add(word);
  }
 }
}

@Override
public void cleanup() {
}
}
```

Now let's see what happens in `UserHashtagJoinBolt`. The first important thing to notice is that it is a `BaseBatchBolt`. This means that the `execute` method will operate on the received tuples but won't be emitting any new tuple. Eventually, when the batch is finished, Storm will call the `finishBatch` method.

```
public void execute(Tuple tuple) {
    String source = tuple.getSourceStreamId();
    String tweetId = tuple.getStringByField("tweet_id");

    if("hashtags".equals(source)) {
      String hashtag = tuple.getStringByField("hashtag");
      add(tweetHashtags, tweetId, hashtag);
    } else if("users".equals(source)) {
      String user = tuple.getStringByField("user");
      add(userTweets, user, tweetId);
    }
}
```

Since you need to associate all the hashtags of a tweet with the users mentioned in that tweet and count how many times they appeared, you need to join the two streams of the previous bolts. Do that for the entire batch, and once it finishes, the `finishBatch` method is called.

```
@Override
public void finishBatch() {

  for (String user : userTweets.keySet()) {
    Set<String> tweets = getUserTweets(user);
    HashMap<String, Integer> hashtagsCounter = new HashMap<String, Integer>();
    for (String tweet : tweets) {
      Set<String> hashtags = getTweetHashtags(tweet);
      if(hashtags != null) {
        for (String hashtag : hashtags) {
          Integer count = hashtagsCounter.get(hashtag);
```

```
      if(count == null)
        count = 0;
      count ++;
      hashtagsCounter.put(hashtag, count);
    }

  }
}

  for (String hashtag : hashtagsCounter.keySet()) {
    int count = hashtagsCounter.get(hashtag);
    collector.emit(new Values(id, user, hashtag, count));
  }
 }
}
```

In this method, generate and emit a tuple for each user-hashtag, and the amount of times it occurred.

You can see the complete implementation in the downloadable code available on Git-Hub (*https://github.com/storm-book/examples-ch08-transactional-topologies*).

The Committer Bolts

As you've learned, batches of tuples are sent by the coordinator and emitters across the topology. Those batched of tuples are processed in parallel without any specific order.

The *coordinator bolts* are special batch bolts that implement ICommitter or have been set with setCommiterBolt in the TransactionalTopologyBuilder. The main difference with regular batch bolts is that the finishBatch method of committer bolts executes when the batch is ready to be committed. This happens when all previous transactions have been committed successfully. Additionally, finishBatch method is executed sequentially. So if the batch with transaction ID 1 and the batch with transaction ID 2 are being processed in parallel in the topology, the finishBatch method of the committer bolt that is processing the batch with transaction ID 2 will get executed only when the finishBatch of batch with transaction ID 1 has finished without any errors.

The implementation of this class follows:

```
public class RedisCommiterCommiterBolt extends BaseTransactionalBolt
    implements ICommitter {
  public static final String LAST_COMMITED_TRANSACTION_FIELD = "LAST_COMMIT";
  TransactionAttempt id;
  BatchOutputCollector collector;
  Jedis jedis;


  @Override
  public void prepare(Map conf, TopologyContext context,
      BatchOutputCollector collector, TransactionAttempt id) {
    this.id = id;
    this.collector = collector;
```

```java
    this.jedis = new Jedis("localhost");
}

HashMap<String, Long> hashtags = new HashMap<String, Long>();
HashMap<String, Long> users = new HashMap<String, Long>();
HashMap<String, Long> usersHashtags = new HashMap<String, Long>();

private void count(HashMap<String, Long> map, String key, int count) {
    Long value = map.get(key);
    if(value == null)
    value = (long) 0;
    value += count;
    map.put(key, value);
}

@Override
public void execute(Tuple tuple) {
    String origin = tuple.getSourceComponent();
    if("users-splitter".equals(origin)) {
        String user = tuple.getStringByField("user");
        count(users, user, 1);
    } else if("hashtag-splitter".equals(origin)) {
        String hashtag = tuple.getStringByField("hashtag");
        count(hashtags, hashtag, 1);
    } else if("user-hashtag-merger".equals(origin)) {
        String hashtag = tuple.getStringByField("hashtag");
        String user = tuple.getStringByField("user");
        String key = user + ":" + hashtag;
        Integer count = tuple.getIntegerByField("count");
        count(usersHashtags, key, count);
    }
}


@Override
public void finishBatch() {
    String lastCommitedTransaction = jedis.get(LAST_COMMITED_TRANSACTION_FIELD);
    String currentTransaction = ""+id.getTransactionId();

    if(currentTransaction.equals(lastCommitedTransaction))
        return ;

    Transaction multi = jedis.multi();

    multi.set(LAST_COMMITED_TRANSACTION_FIELD, currentTransaction);

    Set<String> keys = hashtags.keySet();
    for (String hashtag : keys) {
        Long count = hashtags.get(hashtag);
        multi.hincrBy("hashtags", hashtag, count);
    }

    keys = users.keySet();
    for (String user : keys) {
        Long count = users.get(user);
```

```
      multi.hincrBy("users", user, count);
    }

    keys = usersHashtags.keySet();
    for (String key : keys) {
      Long count = usersHashtags.get(key);
      multi.hincrBy("users_hashtags", key, count);
    }

    multi.exec();
  }

  @Override
  public void declareOutputFields(OutputFieldsDeclarer declarer) {
  }
}
```

This is all very straightforward, but there is a very important detail in the `finishBatch` method.

```
    ...
    multi.set(LAST_COMMITED_TRANSACTION_FIELD, currentTransaction);
    ...
```

Here you are storing in your database the last transaction ID committed. Why should you do that? Remember that if a transaction fails, Storm will be replaying it as many times as necessary. If you don't make sure that you already processed the transaction, you could overcount and the whole idea of a transactional topology would be useless. So remember: *store the last transaction ID committed and check against it before committing.*

Partitioned Transactional Spouts

It is very common for a spout to read batches of tuples from a set of partitions. Continuing the example, you could have several Redis databases and the tweets could be split across those Redis databases. By implementing `IPartitionedTransactionalSpout`, Storm offers some facilities to manage the state for every partition and guarantee the ability to replay.

Let's see how to modify your previous `TweetsTransactionalSpout` so it can handle partitions.

First, extend `BasePartitionedTransactionalSpout`, which implements `IPartitionedTransactionalSpout`.

```
    public class TweetsPartitionedTransactionalSpout extends
            BasePartitionedTransactionalSpout<TransactionMetadata> {
    ...
    }
```

Tell Storm, which is your coordinator.

```java
public static class TweetsPartitionedTransactionalCoordinator implements Coordinator {
  @Override
  public int numPartitions() {
    return 4;
  }

  @Override
  public boolean isReady() {
    return true;
  }

  @Override
  public void close() {
  }
}
```

In this case, the coordinator is very simple. In the numPartitions method, tell Storm
how many partitions you have. And also notice that you don't return any metadata. In
an IPartitionedTransactionalSpout, the metadata is managed by the emitter directly.

Let's see how the emitter is implemented.

```java
public static class TweetsPartitionedTransactionalEmitter
        implements Emitter<TransactionMetadata> {
  PartitionedRQ rq = new PartitionedRQ();

  @Override
  public TransactionMetadata emitPartitionBatchNew(TransactionAttempt tx,
        BatchOutputCollector collector, int partition,
        TransactionMetadata lastPartitionMeta) {
    long nextRead;

    if(lastPartitionMeta == null)
      nextRead = rq.getNextRead(partition);
    else {
      nextRead = lastPartitionMeta.from + lastPartitionMeta.quantity;
      rq.setNextRead(partition, nextRead); // Move the cursor
    }

    long quantity = rq.getAvailableToRead(partition, nextRead);
    quantity = quantity > MAX_TRANSACTION_SIZE ? MAX_TRANSACTION_SIZE : quantity;
    TransactionMetadata metadata = new TransactionMetadata(nextRead, (int)quantity);

    emitPartitionBatch(tx, collector, partition, metadata);
    return metadata;
  }

  @Override
  public void emitPartitionBatch(TransactionAttempt tx, BatchOutputCollector
collector,
        int partition, TransactionMetadata partitionMeta) {
    if(partitionMeta.quantity <= 0)
      return ;

    List<String> messages = rq.getMessages(partition, partitionMeta.from,
        partitionMeta.quantity);
```

```
        long tweetId = partitionMeta.from;
        for (String msg : messages) {
          collector.emit(new Values(tx, ""+tweetId, msg));
          tweetId ++;
        }
      }

      @Override
      public void close() {
      }
    }
```

There are two important methods here, `emitPartitionBatchNew` and `emitPartition` `Batch`. In `emitPartitionBatch`, you receive from Storm the `partition` parameter, which tells you which partition you should retrieve the batch of tuples from. In this method, decide which tweets to retrieve, generate the corresponding metadata, call `emitParti` `tionBatch`, and return the metadata, which will be stored immediately in Zookeeper.

Storm will send the same transaction ID for every partition, as the transaction exists across all the partitions. Read from the partition the tweets in the `emitPartition` `Batch` method, and emit the tuples of the batch to the topology. If the batch fails, Storm will call `emitPartitionBatch` with the stored metadata to replay the batch.

 You can check the code at ch08-transactional topologies on GitHub (*https://github.com/storm-book/examples-ch08-transactional-topolo gies*).

Opaque Transactional Topologies

So far, you might have assumed that it's always possible to replay a batch of tuples for the same transaction ID. But that might not be feasible in some scenarios. What happens then?

It turns out that you can still achieve exactly once semantics, but it requires some more development effort as you will need to keep previous state in case the transaction is replayed by Storm. Since you can get different tuples for the same transaction ID, when emitting in different moments in time, you'll need to reset to that previous state and go from there.

For example, if you are counting total received tweets, you have currently counted five and in the last transaction, with ID 321, you count eight more. You would keep those three values—`previousCount=5`, `currentCount=13`, and `lastTransactionId=321`. In case transaction ID 321 is emitted again and since you get different tuples, you count four more instead of eight, the committer will detect that is the same transaction ID, it would reset to the `previousCount` of five, and will add those new four and update `current` `Count` to nine.

Also, every transaction that is being processed in parallel will be cancelled when a previous transaction in cancelled. This is to ensure that you don't miss anything in the middle.

Your spout should implement IOpaquePartitionedTransactionalSpout and as you can see, the coordinator and emitters are very simple.

```
public static class TweetsOpaquePartitionedTransactionalSpoutCoordinator implements
IOpaquePartitionedTransactionalSpout.Coordinator {
  @Override
  public boolean isReady() {
    return true;
  }
}
```

```
public static class TweetsOpaquePartitionedTransactionalSpoutEmitter implements
IOpaquePartitionedTransactionalSpout.Emitter<TransactionMetadata> {
  PartitionedRQ rq = new PartitionedRQ();

  @Override
  public TransactionMetadata emitPartitionBatch(TransactionAttempt tx,
      BatchOutputCollector collector, int partition,
      TransactionMetadata lastPartitionMeta) {
    long nextRead;

    if(lastPartitionMeta == null)
      nextRead = rq.getNextRead(partition);
    else {
      nextRead = lastPartitionMeta.from + lastPartitionMeta.quantity;
      rq.setNextRead(partition, nextRead); // Move the cursor
    }

    long quantity = rq.getAvailableToRead(partition, nextRead);
    quantity = quantity > MAX_TRANSACTION_SIZE ? MAX_TRANSACTION_SIZE : quantity;
    TransactionMetadata metadata = new TransactionMetadata(nextRead, (int)quantity);
    emitMessages(tx, collector, partition, metadata);
    return metadata;
  }


  private void emitMessages(TransactionAttempt tx, BatchOutputCollector collector,
        int partition, TransactionMetadata partitionMeta) {
    if(partitionMeta.quantity <= 0)
      return ;

    List<String> messages =
        rq.getMessages(partition, partitionMeta.from, partitionMeta.quantity);
    long tweetId = partitionMeta.from;
    for (String msg : messages) {
      collector.emit(new Values(tx, ""+tweetId, msg));
      tweetId ++;
    }
  }

  @Override
```

```
    public int numPartitions() {
      return 4;
    }

    @Override
    public void close() {
    }
}
```

The most interesting method is emitPartitionBatch, which receives the previous committed metadata. You should use that information to generate a batch of tuples. This
batch won't be necessarily the same, as was said earlier, you might not be able to re-
produce the same batch. The rest of the job is handled by the committer bolts, which
use the previous state.

Installing the Storm Client

The Storm client will enable you to use the commands to manage topologies into a cluster. To install the Storm client, follow these steps:

1. Download the latest stable version from the Storm site (*https://github.com/nathan marz/storm/downloads*) at this moment the latest version is storm-0.6.2.

2. Once you've downloaded the version, unzip it into the */usr/local/bin/storm* to have storm in a shared directory.

3. Next, add the storm binary PATH variable to be able to run the storm command without having to put the complete path, if we've used the */usr/local/bin/storm* directory, the command will be *export PATH=$PATH:/usr/local/bin/storm*.

4. After that, you need to create a Storm local configuration where you'll say which is your nimbus host. To do it, create a file in *~/.storm/storm.yaml* with the following content:

```
nimbus.host: "our nimbus address"
```

Now, you have the needed to manage topologies in your Storm cluster.

 The Storm client contains all the storm commands needed to run a Storm cluster, but to run it you need to install other tools and configure some params. See how to do that into the Appendix B.

To manage the topologies into the cluster, you have a bunch of very simple and useful commands that allow you to submit, kill, disable, re-enable, and rebalance our topology.

The jar command is responsible for executing your topology and submitting it to the cluster through the StormSubmitter object into the main class.

```
storm jar path-to-topology-jar class-with-the-main arg1 arg2 argN
```

path-to-topology-jar is the complete path to the compiled jar where your topology code and all your libraries are. The *class-with-the-main* will be the main place where the StormSubmitter is executed and the rest of arguments will be the params that receive our main method.

With Storm you have the capability to *suspend* or *disable* a running topology, deactivating the topology spouts, so when we deactivate the topology, all emitted tuples will be processed, but the *nextTuple* method of the topology spouts will not be called.

To disable a topology, run:

```
storm deactivate topology-name
```

If you want re-activate a disabled topology, run:

```
storm activate topology-name
```

If you want to destroy a topology, you can use the `kill` command. This will destroy the topology in a secure fashion, disabling the topology first and waiting for the duration of the topology's message, allowing the topology to finish the process of the current streams.

To kill a topology, run:

```
storm kill topology-name
```

You can change the waiting time after the topology is deactivated using the `-w [time-in-sec]` parameter when you run the Storm kill command.

Rebalance enables you to redistribute the tasks through all worker tasks into a cluster. This is a powerful command when you have not balanced your tasks. For example, when you add nodes to a running cluster. The rebalance command will deactivate the topology for the duration of message timeout and redistribute the workers so Storm will re-activate the topology.

To rebalance a topology, run:

```
storm rebalance topology-name
```

If you want to use another deactivation duration, you could use the `-w` parameter to set it:

```
storm rebalance topology-name -w other-time
```

You can see the complete list of Storm commands by running the Storm client without parameters. The complete description of these commands can be found at *https://github.com/nathanmarz/storm/wiki/Command-line-client*.

Installing Storm Cluster

If you want to create a Storm cluster, there are two ways to do so:

- Use storm-deploy (*https://github.com/nathanmarz/storm-deploy*) to create a cluster on Amazon EC2, as you saw in Chapter 6.
- Install Storm manually (more on this in this Appendix).

To install Storm manually, install:

- Zookeeper cluster (see how in the Administration Guide (*http://zookeeper.apache .org/doc/r3.3.3/zookeeperAdmin.html*))
- Java 6.0
- Python 2.6.6
- Unzip command

 All of the following steps, the Java, Python and unzip commands will be required in Nimbus and the supervisor process.

When you've met the requirements, install the native libraries.

To install ZeroMQ, run:

```
wget http://download.zeromq.org/historic/zeromq-2.1.7.tar.gz
tar -xzf zeromq-2.1.7.tar.gz
cd zeromq-2.1.7
./configure
make
sudo make install
```

To install JZMQ, run:

```
git clone https://github.com/nathanmarz/jzmq.git
cd jzmq
./autogen.sh
./configure
```

```
    make
    sudo make install
```

Once you have installed the native libraries, download the latest Storm stable version (Storm 0.7.1 at the time of this writing), and unzip it.

Modify the configuration file to add your Storm cluster configuration (you can see all default configurations on defaults.yaml (*https://github.com/nathanmarz/storm/blob/master/conf/defaults.yaml*) in the Storm repository).

To modify the storm cluster configuration, you'll need to edit the *conf/storm.yaml* file located in the Storm folder and set (at least) the following parameters:

```
storm.zookeeper.servers:
  - "zookeeper addres 1"
  - "zookeeper addres 2"
  - "zookeeper addres N"

storm.local.dir: "a local directory"

nimbus.host: "Numbus host addres"

supervisor.slots.ports:
  - supervisor slot port 1
  - supervisor slot port 2
  - supervisor slot port N
```

The parameters are the following:

storm.zookeeper.servers
    The address of your zookeeper servers.

storm.local.dir
    A local directory where the Storm process will store internal data. (It's very important that the user who runs the storm process has write access over this directory.)

nimbus.host
    The address of the machine where the Nimbus will run.

supervisor.slots.ports
    The ports (normally starting on 6700) that the workers use for receiving messages; the supervisor will run one worker per port declared into this property.

When you've configured these parameters, you can run all the Storm processes. If you want to do a local test, you can configure *nimbus.host* to localhost.

To start one process, run into the Storm folder: *./bin/storm process name.*

Storm comes with an excellent utility called Storm UI, which enables you to monitor your topologies.

Real Life Example Setup

First, clone the GitHub repository for the example from:

```
> git clone git://github.com/storm-book/examples-ch06-real-life-app.git
```

src/main
> Contains the *Topology* souce code

src/test
> Has the tests for the *Topology*

webapps directory h
> Has the Node.Js WebApp to play with the *Topology*

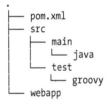

```
├── pom.xml
├── src
│   ├── main
│   │   └── java
│   └── test
│       └── groovy
└── webapp
```

Installing Redis

Installing Redis is very easy:

1. Download the latest stable version from the Redis website (*http://redis.io/down load*) (at the time of this writing, 2.4.14).
2. Extract the file.
3. Run `make`, followed by `make install`.

This will compile Redis and leave executable files in your PATH so you can start using Redis.

You'll find more information on the Redis website as well as documentation on commands and design considerations.

Installing Node.js

Installing Node.js is pretty straightforward. Download the latest Node.js source from *http://www.nodejs.org/#download*.

At the time of this writing, the latest version of NodeJS is *0.6.19*. Extract the content of the file and run `./configure`, `make`, and `make install`.

You'll find more information on the official site, as well as documentation on how to install Node.js on different platforms.

Building and Testing

In order to build the example, you should start the *redis-server* on your machine.

```
>nohup redis-server &
```

After that, run the *mvn* command to effectively compile and test the application.

```
>mvn package
...
[INFO] ------------------------------------------------------------------------
[INFO] BUILD SUCCESS
[INFO] ------------------------------------------------------------------------
[INFO] Total time: 32.163s
[INFO] Finished at: Sun Jun 17 18:55:10 GMT-03:00 2012
[INFO] Final Memory: 9M/81M
[INFO] ------------------------------------------------------------------------
>
```

Running the Topology

Once the *redis-server* is running and the build is successful, start the topology running in a *LocalCluster*.

```
>java -jar target/storm-analytics-0.0.1-jar-with-dependencies.jar
```

After the topology is started, you can start the *Node.js Web Application* by running the following:

```
>node webapp/app.js
```

 Topology and Node.js commands block eachother. Try running them in different terminals.

Playing with the Example

Type *http://localhost:3000/* and start playing with the example!

About the Authors

Jonathan Leibiusky, Head of Research and Development at MercadoLibre, has been working in software development for more than 10 years. He has developed and contributed to several new and existing open source projects, including "Jedis", which is being used actively by VMware and SpringSource.

Gabriel Eisbruch is a computer science student who has been working as a Software Architect in Mercadolibre (NASDAQ MELI) since 2007. He is tasked with researching technologies and developing projects. In the last year, he has specialized in big data analysis, implementing MercadoLibre's Hadoop cluster.

Dario Simonassi has been working in software development for more than 10 years. Since 2004, he has specialized in large website operations and performance. Today Dario is the Chief Architect of MercadoLibre (NASDAQ MELI) where he leads the architecture team.

Have it your way.

Lightning Source UK Ltd.
Milton Keynes UK
UKHW032108290921
391396UK00009B/415